CLASS A
TRANSFORMATIONAL
JOURNEY

OLIVER WIGHT

Class A Business Excellence
For

✓ Managing the Strategic Planning Process
✓ Managing and Leading People
✓ Driving Business Improvement
✓ Integrated Business Planning
✓ Managing the Products and Services Portfolio
✓ Managing Market Demand
✓ Managing the Supply Chain
✓ Managing Internal Supply
✓ Managing External Sourcing

The Oliver Wight
Class A Standard for
Business Excellence

The Oliver Wight Class A Standard for Business Excellence

SEVENTH EDITION

WILEY

ISBN 9781119404477 (paper); ISBN 9781119404484 (ePDF); ISBN 9781119404491 (ePub)

Printed in the United States of America

10 9 8 7 6 5 4 3 2 1

CONTENTS

Additional clarification can be obtained from the Oliver Wight International website (www.oliverwight.com), where a glossary and the definitions to support Performance Measurements can be found.

PREFACE

Welcome to the seventh edition of *The Oliver Wight Class A Standard for Business Excellence*.

The seventh edition continues our focus on Business Excellence. It describes the distinguishing characteristics of the high-performing companies, how these attributes were achieved and, important, how they are sustained. The answers were gathered from the accumulated experiences of the Oliver Wight global group and their relationships with thousands of successful businesses. The outcome is a new standard for evaluating business excellence at your company.

For those executives challenged to raise their companies' level of performance, doing so starts with a commitment to a long-term journey, strategically focused and supported with a series of improvement programs. Each program has a milestone marking its achievement. Collectively, they lead to *The Oliver Wight Class A Standard for Business Excellence*.

In the 1970s, Ollie created the first checklist. The test of what to include remains the same; in the hands of educated users, do they produce the desired results? Only proven, practical solutions become standards.

Many folks have contributed to the know-how in this book. Deserving special recognition are:

Andrew Purton as its champion
Lloyd Snowden, the driving force

Lloyd Snowden, Andrew Purton, Jim Correll, Jon Minerich, Mike Reed, and Susan Hansen provided the global leadership.

Each chapter had contributors: Paul Archer, Debbie Bowen-Heaton, Les Brookes, Stephen Bucksey, Zoe Davis, Eric Deutsch, Paul Ducie, Michael Effron, Todd Ferguson, Mike Gray, David Goddard, Susan Hansen, Stuart Harman, Anne Hilton, Robert Hirschey, Robert Howard, Dawn Howarth, Rod Hozack, Anne-Marie Kilkenny, Stewart Kelly, Donald McNaughton, Peter Metcalfe, Jon Minerich, Andrew Purton,

Mike Reed, Timm Reiher, Jerry Shanahan, Lloyd Snowden, Jason Stanton, and Andrew Walker.

For those executives eager to take up the challenge of raising their companies' performance to heights of excellence, this standard will show them the way.

—Walt Goddard
Chairman Emeritus,
Oliver Wight International, Inc.

INTRODUCTION

This seventh edition of *The Oliver Wight Class A Standard for Business Excellence* follows the same structure as the previous edition but has transitioned from a checklist format to focus solely on the characteristics of Business Excellence—the *Standard*. This is in recognition that, for most businesses, the quest to attain the Business Excellence standard is a transformational journey, not a single initiative but a series of improvement programs known as Class A Milestones to facilitate the journey. The milestones are based on the elements in the *Standard* required to support the business objective to be achieved. Oliver Wight has created a series of workbooks designed to define typical Class A Milestones. The *Standard* and the workbooks answer the *what* required for Business Excellence. The *how* is answered through the Oliver Wight Proven Path for Business Transformation, which is founded on best-practice education, facilitated workshops to apply best practices to specific businesses, and implementation coaching.

The Journey to Business Excellence is demanding, and this latest edition has been updated to address changes in business practices since the sixth edition was updated in 2010. Moreover, the changes in business expectations continue apace. Companies holding back from keeping up with the pack may be found wanting in the race to win in business.

WINNING WITH CLASS A

Every company that achieves a Class A Milestone is rewarded with bottom-line results and an energized and empowered workforce—life gets better, if for no other reason than completing the day with a feeling of accomplishment. Achieving a Class A Milestone takes more than just this *Standard*. Having worked with companies on Class A since 1978, we recognize what is required to be successful. It isn't as simple as buying a book and then setting out to meet the requirements. The seven steps for success are:

1. The *Standard*—describes the Business Excellence benchmark.
2. The *Proven Path*—a proven approach to delivering business transformation. This includes the *why* we need to do this; *what* we are going to do, in prioritized sequence, to support a journey; and the *how* to implement sustainably.

3. Milestone Workbooks—describe the *what* for a specific milestone along the journey.
4. Education—explains the *what* and the *how*, in detail, for each element of the *Standard* associated with a milestone.
5. Application Workshops—address the *how* to apply these practices tailored to your specific business and organization requirements.
6. Coaching—supports your people on the *how* to handle the specific issues and challenges of milestone activities and the crucial change management requirements.
7. Celebration—recognition for the successful completion of a milestone.

SCOPE OF THE STANDARD

The *Standard* encompasses all business sectors and business processes. Manufacturing and service sectors are growing closer together in their characteristics. In many ways, the new best-practice manufacturing companies may be considered service companies but whose service is to sell products. Business differentiators have moved to managing products and services, managing the supply chain (often without manufacturing any of the product), managing the procurement of externally sourced items, and developing more effective relationships with employees, suppliers, customers, and consumers. All these dimensions are extensively covered, alongside the more traditional foundation elements you would expect to find in the *Standard* for Business Excellence. Further technology advances now permit dynamic business management, where business performance, including financials, can be reviewed daily and where agility permits the business to respond and move with market forces in days, not weeks or months.

THE CHAPTERS

At the start of each chapter, a Purpose statement describes the purpose and scope of the chapter process. There is also a Positioning statement in recognition that we are not attempting to describe the characteristics of every transition in maturity. This *Standard* consists of defining characteristics, competencies, and performance requirements of a business positioned toward the top of Phase 2 of the Business Maturity Map (see Foundation, Figure I.1). Many good practices developed in Phase 1 are now assumed rather than expressed while, in other cases, there is a transition of processes and roles from Phase 1 to Phase 2. The Phase 1 characteristics and performance requirements are captured in the respective Phase 1 Milestone Workbooks, not in this *Standard*. Please read the Positioning statement so that you are orientated to understand which characteristics, behaviors, capabilities, performance levels, and organizational challenges have already been addressed in Phase 1 before reading the new or continued requirements of Phase 2.

The chapter structure in the *Standard* is aligned with the Integrated Business Model. It begins with "Managing the Strategic Planning Process" as the driver of the business, followed by the two enabling disciplines of "Managing and Leading People" and "Driving Business Improvement." Chapters 4 through 9 address the core processes, commencing with Integrated Business Planning.

- **Managing the Strategic Planning Process:** The business Vision and Strategic Plan need to be explicit so that your people have clear direction for their plans and activities. This chapter will challenge your process for longer-term planning of the business. It will demand the setting of business priorities and clear communication when deploying your plans and your Business Excellence program throughout the business.

- **Managing and Leading People:** People are the ultimate differentiator as business gets more competitive and markets more demanding. This chapter will require you to think through your business values and how you are organized for the tasks ahead; that you are clear about the company culture and behaviors that you need; and that you have active development programs designed to improve the competencies of your people for the new challenges ahead. It will also challenge your processes for knowledge management and your culture of Leadership and Teamwork.

- **Driving Business Improvement:** This articulates the maturity of your business improvement processes. It then challenges how you prioritize your Business Improvement programs to achieve the early gains in areas that create a solid foundation for the future. You'll be challenged to walk before you try to run and to give value to those everyday issues that are at the heart of excellence in business.

- **Integrated Business Planning:** Integrated Business Planning (IBP) is the business management process driving in strategy deployment and optimized business performance and, thereby, directs revenue and earnings-generating activities.

  At the foundation of IBP is Sales & Operations Planning (S&OP), originally developed by Oliver Wight as a vehicle to engage the Senior Management Team in integrated management of the Supply Chain.

  The IBP process is becoming the unique and, increasingly, the de facto best-practice approach to deploy business strategy and manage integration with day-to-day activity; it is the prime tool for keeping all parts of the company on a common agenda and set of priorities; and it manages the entire business through one set of numbers— dynamically tuned to the latest market situation that ensures timely actions to maintain management control of business performance. IBP provides long-term visibility and, through modeling and rigorous risk management tools, enables optimized outcomes with suitable contingency planning.

- **Managing the Products and Services Portfolio:** In every business sector, product life cycles are shortening. Portfolios should represent the optimization of products and services, including appropriate introduction of new and carefully planned phase-out of old. This chapter challenges how well and how fast you align your portfolio and monitor the performance of products and services. Your clear Technology Roadmap supports this and, when applicable, includes prototyping to increase the speed to market. The portfolio is managed to ensure margin development, but when this becomes a problem, the Strategic Plan, Product and Portfolio Roadmap, and processes are challenged to introduce changes to enable sustainable positive margins. It expects the deployment of the latest practices in program and project management supported by computer-aided risk management and decision making to anticipate and avoid adverse consequences.

- **Managing Market Demand:** Greater understanding of customer and consumer needs and of what is happening in your marketplace, when applied effectively, leads directly to increased predictability throughout the business horizon. Knowing your market enables better planning of your position, with more successful order-winning plans and activities. These plans are directed by the Strategic Market Roadmap which, in turn, drives Market Segmentation Roadmaps to address the needs of homogeneous customer and consumer groups specifically. This chapter challenges your development of analytics and predictive modeling and how close you are to real demand knowledge. The chapter ensures a focus on demand plan creation and accuracy and how professionally you control supply and demand in the very short term through a demand-sensing capability and execution of sales activity driving a demand-led Supply Chain.

- **Managing the Supply Chain:** As the latest technology extends our target market, the increasing challenge to business is how to deliver the portfolios of products and services to the point of use. This chapter challenges how well your Supply Chain Roadmap and delivery capability are optimized through a collaborative supply network and segmentation. Advanced Planning techniques are deployed to achieve Agile customer service and Class A business performance.

- **Managing Internal Supply:** Business today has moved to the management of a fully integrated and collaborative Supply Chain. Excellence in core supply activities is vital to ensure requests from customers and consumers are satisfied and, at the same time, meet the challenge of global cost competition. This chapter challenges every aspect of your Internal Supply capability, its adoption of excellence, and how quickly it must respond to changes in demand, market, and competitive pressures.

- **Managing External Sourcing:** The optimization of products and services, and ever-more sophisticated market dynamics present new challenges to make/buy decisions. They also impact External Sourcing Roadmaps that align with Supply Chain decisions on segmentation and collaboration. Technology offers new procurement approaches that have major potential for saving, and this has significantly advanced the use of Total Cost of Ownership in critical decision making. This chapter sets new standards for assessing excellence in your procurement processes and ensures the values of the business are maintained externally through an ethical approach to supplier selection and management.

PERFORMANCE MEASUREMENTS

Performance Measures are identified within each chapter, but we have not always specified absolute requirements or metrics. At the level of business maturity represented by the *Standard*, we expect Performance Measurement to be relevant to delivery of your strategy and, thereby, specific to each business. Typical performance measures are identified and defined in the individual workbooks for the appropriate milestone.

THE IMPORTANCE OF PEOPLE

Class A starts with people. To be more effective and productive, you must implement new practices (people, processes, and tools) into the company. Your people create the processes but, to be effective, it is crucial that the required behaviors are recognized and designed into new practices. Your people also select or design the tools to enable these new practices. Fundamentally, all users and participants must then be educated (why) and trained (how) on their use, but sadly there is often under-investment in this crucial internal education and training activity. Without the disciplined integration of people, processes, and tools, your designed practices will not drive the desired improvement.

You will also be challenged to manage integrated processes rather than perform in functional silos. These processes will need people to work together in a team-based culture of multiple disciplines and functions, and your people will face ever-more complex tools with which to run the business. People are your biggest business differentiator now and will be more so as your excellence program matures. Treasure, develop, and educate them. They are the future.

CELEBRATION

Milestone programs will not only substantially improve business performance but will act as catalysts for Business Transformation. It is important at the completion of key milestones on the business journey that Leadership steps back and celebrates contributions and successes. By taking the time to celebrate the completion of a milestone, the company can both recognize the magnitude of the improvement journey to date, and satisfy and leverage the need for recognition. It is like any sporting event—it may be fun to play the game, but it is a lot more fun when you win. Celebrations should be something people look forward to—they will energize and motivate. This is extremely important when you are on a Class A Journey. As success both in business results and team achievement builds, so will the enthusiasm for tackling future milestones.

MILESTONES ON THE JOURNEY TO EXCELLENCE

The Class A *Standard* achievement is extremely demanding (and rewarding) and typically requires a long period for implementation. When you start the Class A Journey to Excellence, we recommend that you outline a Business Excellence program aligned to strategic and competitive priorities. Design incremental milestone initiatives to provide business gains in a relatively short timescale while taking you a step further toward those longer-term business goals. Milestones enable the Journey to Class A and serve as major points of recognition of your people. Oliver Wight recognizes the achievement of these milestones and their deliverables with a Class A Milestone Award.

Oliver Wight Class A Milestone Awards come in three forms:

- **Oliver Wight Class A:** The full Class A award when an entire enterprise meets the requirements of all chapters of this *Standard.*
- **Oliver Wight Business Unit Class A Accreditation:** To recognize the achievements of a stand-alone business within a larger multi-entity enterprise that meets all the requirements of its appropriate scope.
- **Oliver Wight Class A Milestone Award:** To recognize successful execution of defined transformation projects that comprise a milestone in your Business Improvement program, with delivered business gains on the Journey to Class A Business Excellence. There is an award for each milestone you achieve.

FOUNDATION

As each day passes, companies in every sector of business get faster, smarter, and more innovative. This is reflected in the updated Class A Standard of Business Excellence. The foundational principles that must be in place for a company to achieve outstanding performance are set out in this section.

THE JOURNEY TO EXCELLENCE

For more detail on the Journey to Excellence, you might want to read the companion volume to the *Standard*, *Achieving Class A Business Excellence: An Executive's Perspective.*

The Journey to Excellence is tough and uncompromising. It is never-ending and is applied to every part and every process in the company. For such a journey to be sustainable, it must continually deliver results and gains for all its stakeholders. The journey is a series of bite-sized projects with reasonable and realistic timescales. These build into longer Business Improvement programs that ensure success now and in the future. Improvement activity must be prioritized to the current needs of stakeholders while delivering the firm foundations for future advanced work. As in building a house, you risk everything if the right foundations are not firmly in place before you continue the program to finish the house.

The Oliver Wight Business Maturity Map (see Figure I.1), supported by Maturity Transitions derived from the *Standard*, enables you to understand the maturity of your business and any gap to Business Excellence. Maturity positioning is established from an Oliver Wight Diagnostic. This understanding will enable the improvement journey to be designed, identifying the required programs and projects, defined by Oliver Wight Milestones, to close the maturity gap.

To support the journey through Phases 1 and 2, Oliver Wight have developed a series of Maturity Transitions that show the five transitions of maturity for core processes and organizational characteristics. These Maturity Transitions are used to specify the 'as is' positioning. Figure I.2 shows an example of the Integrated Business Planning Maturity Transition.

Figure I.1   The Oliver Wight Business Maturity Map and Phases

Oliver Wight address how to achieve the standards through Education, which is arranged both publicly and privately in all parts of the world, followed by facilitated Application Workshops. Finally, Oliver Wight supports the detailed implementation activities and Change Management dynamics through Coaching.

It must be stressed that excellence is not doing what you do today better. It means adopting new processes and, likely, a different enabling culture: a shift to a more effective and dynamic paradigm. This shift occurs through a series of maturity phases.

Phase 1: Instead of living with firefighting or even thriving on it, you must address the root cause of firefighting or reactive (even knee-jerk) management in your business. Unplanned events may be driven from the marketplace because your customers require more than your current processes can deliver, or they may arise from your own in-house, undisciplined way of working and your associated behaviors. Left unresolved, firefighting drains management time and energy in solving the same issues over and over. It prevents gains from problem solving and team-based initiatives being sustained. Tackling the root causes behind being event driven, while applying good practice principles, constitutes Phase 1 of your Journey to Excellence: "Eliminating unplanned events and doing routine things routinely." (See Phase 1 in Figure I.1.) With the foundation of a well-planned and coordinated business in place, you are ready for the next phase.

Phase 2: Your prioritized business needs and the need to accelerate your processes, making them more reliable and agile by eliminating failure and waste, will enable a collaborative and integrated Supply Chain. Sustainability is achieved through capturing the knowledge and experience of your people, at all levels, into processes and procedures

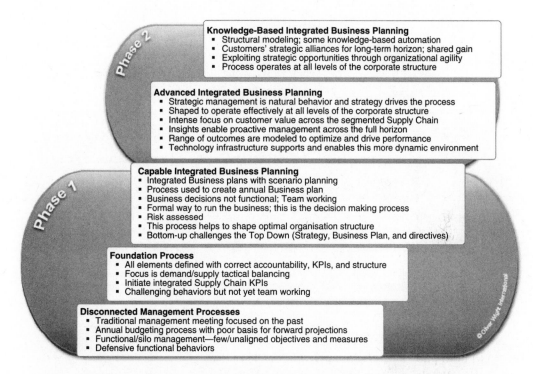

Figure I.2 Oliver Wight Maturity Transitions for Integrated Business Planning

so that it is not lost, should people move on. Focus on the transition from functional to complete business processes; implementation of a team-based culture, elimination of waste, and capture of knowledge are the main elements of Phase 2. This *Standard* defines the processes, team behaviors, activities, and performance required of a Class A company positioned toward the top of Phase 2 Maturity.

Phases 3 and 4: Seek a step change in productivity and effectiveness by implanting this accumulated knowledge of the business into its systems and machines. Increasingly, those systems become more intelligent and require less and less human intervention in decision making. People play a more vital role as knowledgeable workers, focusing on the integrity and management of sophisticated processes and leading innovation to even higher performance. These phases are not about the number and sophistication of computers or computer-controlled machines in your operations, but they do involve the latest information technology to aid knowledge management, modeling, and real-time decision making and communication. They are about your confidence that those systematized practices (people, processes, and tools) will enable the right decisions in all circumstances.

Characteristics of Phases 3 and 4 are not yet included in this *Standard*; however, the standards included ensure that you will be well prepared for them.

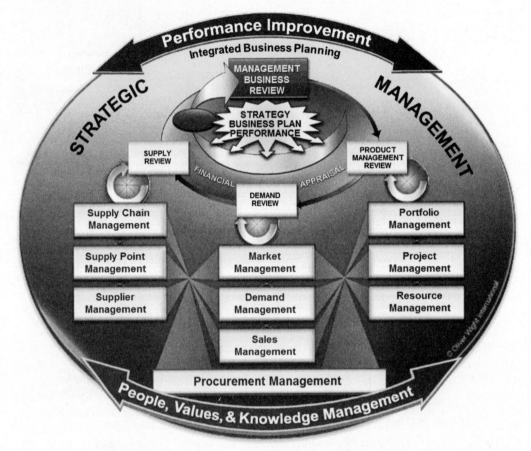

Figure I.3   The Oliver Wight Integrated Business Model

THE INTEGRATED BUSINESS MODEL

The Oliver Wight Integrated Business Model is shown in Figure I.3. It is powered by strategically driven Integrated Business Planning; supported by the core operational processes for product and portfolio, demand, supply, and external sourcing; and enabled by people and behavioral dynamics and business improvement techniques.

Moreover, technology increasingly enables modeling to best optimize the business. A fully deployed, technology-enabled, mature Integrated Business Model (see Figure I.3) operating across the enterprise is the mission of Enterprise Integrated Business Planning (EIBP).

The chapter structure in the *Standard* is aligned to all elements of this Integrated Business Model.

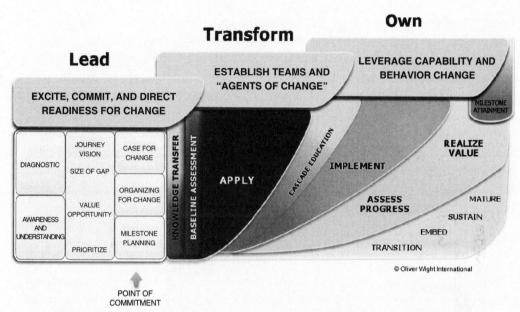

Figure I.4 The Oliver Wight Proven Path for Business Transformation

DELIVERING BUSINESS TRANSFORMATION

Implementing change and delivering true Business Transformation are challenging, and many companies are unsuccessful in this quest. Oliver Wight has the experience of working with thousands of clients over a 40-year history and consultants have created and refined our Change Management methodology. This is called The Proven Path for Business Transformation (see Figure I.4): a step-by-step model for successful Business Transformation.

The Lead Phase

It is critical to secure leadership from Business Executives for any Business Transformation program. They must be excited about the opportunity for the business if they are going to commit, direct, and provide the necessary demonstrated leadership for change.

The Lead phase starts with a Diagnostic or Business Health Check to determine the 'as is' business practices and, hence, business maturity across a specified scope of the business. Findings are reviewed with the Leadership Team within a context of best-practice education to provide awareness and understanding to illustrate business gaps and opportunities. This will enable a fundamental discussion on the size of the gap and the business value opportunity in closing the gap. Can this be achieved in one step or a succession of prioritized improvement programs? Hence, a Journey Vision is created.

Once this clarity is established, work can take place on the Case for Change and how to Organize for Change. This will include (a) required resources: executive process owners as sponsors, project organization, and cross-functional design teams; (b) communication to articulate the case for change, to enroll and mobilize the critical mass of key influencers who will be active in the design; and (c) definition of the suite of measures by which success will be judged. The project plan will define key milestone planning to drive early adoption and time-to-results. As these latter activities approach conclusion, the Leadership Team needs to make a formal decision to proceed. We refer to this as the Point of Commitment.

The Transform Phase

In this phase, business practices are redesigned driven by expectations and criteria expressed in the Lead phase. It commences with Knowledge Transfer where the critical mass of cross-functional key influencers, including executive sponsors, are educated in best practices. Through interactive breakouts, they start to establish their articulation of gaps and opportunities. Supplemented by the diagnostic findings, a Baseline Assessment captures the starting maturity and status of practices. This uses the *Oliver Wight Standard*, expressed at the appropriate level of maturity, in checklist format through a Milestone Workbook. Redesign activity of business practices is conducted through a series of Oliver Wight–facilitated Application Workshops where design teams apply the best-practice principles and characteristics, in which they have been educated, to the nature of the business, recognizing its industry segment foci, geographic footprint, organizational structure, and cultural diversity.

Although process design and supporting systems' functionality is a key focus of design, these must be addressed alongside the behaviors necessary to enable such processes and the required change to ensure behaviors are appropriately driven. Similarly, it is vital to identify old processes, meetings, behaviors, and performance measures that will be eliminated to avoid duplication, confusion, and the undermining of these new practices. With follow-on actions and Design Team Reviews, the Transform phase concludes with a Critical Design Review where the Leadership Steering Team signs off on the design and authorizes deployment.

Through this phase, expertise has been transitioned from Oliver Wight, as the experts in best practice, to the Design Teams, as experts in how Oliver Wight best practices have been applied to the business. As such, these teams, comprising a critical mass of key business influencers, become a critical mass of Agents of Change for these new business practices.

The Own Phase

Following sign-off, the newly designed practices are implemented throughout the organization to leverage capability and behavior change. This phase starts with Cascade Education: a sequence of internal workshops for all participants that builds upon the communication program that has been running throughout the implementation. These sessions are led by Line Managers and Agents of Change to ensure organizational accountability for new practices is expressed, discussed, and internalized, leading to acceptance.

Implementation of designed practices follows, and this is where Oliver Wight coaching support becomes a catalyst for change, stimulating momentum by supporting teams and key sponsors through their change loop and learning curve.

The checklist content within the Milestone Workbooks enables accountable teams to track and assess progress, update gap-closure plans, and score current performance as they strive to deliver the necessary capability associated with their scope of activity. Such progress is confirmed and calibrated through coaching visits and formal checkpoint reviews. As such, Class A Milestones become an important vehicle for change, coordinating the activities of multiple teams though a single integrated program. Because capability improvement is directly linked to process and business performance improvement, progress against milestone criteria will yield value for the business.

Coaching and use of a milestone structure enable movement through the Maturity Transitions, embedding new practices that, through focus and driven by Performance Measures, will deliver sustainable practices. At the appropriate time, the Milestone Assessment is completed, success is celebrated, and the business is ready for its next step in the journey.

Although most companies deliberately set out on a change program, following the Proven Path approach will usually deliver something far more profound—Business Transformation!

1
MANAGING THE STRATEGIC PLANNING PROCESS

PURPOSE

To establish and manage the process for setting vision, strategy, and direction to be a Class A company and improve the company's competitive position. To ensure the strategy is reflected through driving and supporting roadmaps that then direct all programs, projects, plans, and actions throughout the company.

POSITIONING

Strategic Planning processes mature over time through education, committed leadership, expert guidance, and improved market, customer, competitor, and business analysis. Many companies begin Class A improvement journeys in a disconnected state, marked by functional silos, defensive behaviors, a disproportionate focus on the past, and a lack of clarity about the future.

The ability for businesses to make swift and trusted decisions is essential. This is enabled through an integrated Strategic Planning process that clearly defines the business direction laid out in driving and supporting roadmaps covering a horizon that typically extends out five years or more.

Done well, Strategic Planning enables a growing ownership of the business direction, challenges, and opportunities. With increased ownership comes improved communication and understanding which, in turn, enables improved, focused decision making through Integrated Business Planning.

The standard for Strategic Planning defined in this chapter is implemented through a Class A Milestone that drives the next level of process maturity.

CHAPTER CONTENT

Understanding and Analyzing the Internal and External Environment

Vision, Mission, and Values

Strategic Plan

Bringing the Future into Today

Strategy Deployment

Evaluation and Control

Business Strategy Management Process

Risk Management

Performance Measurement

Behaviors and Competencies

UNDERSTANDING AND ANALYZING THE INTERNAL AND EXTERNAL ENVIRONMENT

1. A process exists to collect relevant information internally and externally to understand the company's products and services portfolio, its marketplace, the competition, and future opportunities.

    a. <u>Company Capability</u>

        Core business processes are analyzed for their capability to ensure the company's offer to the marketplace and its Value Proposition. Strengths and weaknesses of these are identified and actions put in place to address them.

    b. <u>Industry Position</u>

        The company actively seeks information and input from inside and outside its sector to benchmark excellent performance in all processes at all levels. It can identify its industry position and, through this understanding, measure how well it performs against a Class A Standard.

    c. <u>Stakeholder Goals</u>

        The major stakeholders in the company are identified, and their short-, medium-, and long-term goals are understood. The company has a balanced view of goals and targets, which are reflected in its driving and supporting roadmaps.

    d. <u>Market Analysis</u>

        Investigation and analysis is carried out to understand the company's markets, its competitors' activity, and the value of its opportunities. This includes geographic focus, consumer and customer demands, economic trends, national and international policies and regulations, etc.

    e. <u>Products and Services Portfolio</u>

        The Products and Services Portfolio is examined to ensure the voice of the customer and consumer are fully reflected in the product strategy. Life-cycle trends identify when portfolio changes are required. The potential of competitor actions, technology developments, and the marketplace are understood and incorporated.

2. **Internal and external information is analyzed using appropriate tools to identify and prioritize opportunities and challenges for the success of the business.**

   a. Information Analysis

   Information is analyzed to determine the future challenges that need to be included in the refreshed Strategic Plan. Potential breakthrough areas for technical and nontechnical innovation are sought and identified for the company to differentiate from its competitors.

   b. Analytical Tools

   Analytical tools are used to model business trends and opportunities and to understand how the company should respond to current and future market needs.

   c. Prioritization

   Opportunities and challenges to meet the business strategy are prioritized using established filter criteria. The potential risk to the business from each opportunity is understood.

VISION, MISSION, AND VALUES

3. **Vision and Mission statements exist, representing the ambitions of the company (or business unit) and its stakeholders.**

   a. Top Down, Team Based

   The company Vision, Mission, and Strategic Plan reflect a horizon appropriate to the business. They are initiated and agreed by the Chief Executive Officer, the company Leadership Team, functional heads, and other key players. They are clearly communicated, understood, and supported by all.

   b. The Vision Statement

   The Vision Statement is inspiring and memorable and summarizes concisely what the company wants to become in its marketplace and community. The Vision for the business is widely communicated in a succinct, consistent, and repeatable way with opportunity for enhancement and feedback.

   c. The Expanded Vision Statement

   The Expanded Vision Statement paints a picture in words and figures to show employees, customers, suppliers, and shareholders what the company plans to become in the medium and long term. It is sufficient to relate their actions and behaviors and their sense of values.

d. The Mission Statement

The Mission Statement is a clear and concise statement of the company's strategic intent. It summarizes the main purpose of the business or business unit and the value that its products and services bring to customers, consumers, and society. It is a clear statement of what the business or unit is here to do.

e. The Expanded Mission Statement

The Expanded Mission Statement explains in words what each of the core process teams needs to do in support of the company Vision. It provides clarity of direction for the core processes and helps develop the core process strategies.

4. The Values are captured in a Value Statement and are lived throughout the company. They shape the driving and supporting strategic roadmaps and supporting programs.

a. Ownership

The Values are owned by the Chief Executive Officer and the Leadership Team and are formally documented in a Values Statement.

b. The Values Statement

The Values, Guiding Principles, and ethics are in use to define how the company will be known. They embody how the company is known by its stakeholders and continue to shape the development of the business culture.

c. Communication

The Values are formally presented to everyone in the company. This ongoing communication process is used to create excitement and purpose, to stimulate behavior change, and to enable value-based challenge regardless of seniority.

d. Living the Values

The leadership of the business visibly demonstrates the Values through their day-to-day behavior and how they engage the organization.

STRATEGIC PLAN

5. A Strategic Plan exists to support the Vision and Mission and clearly articulates the Strategic Business Objectives. It enables the alignment of all processes and plans and is used to direct the development of roadmaps, a measurements hierarchy, and organizational developments, including roles.

   a. The Strategic Plan

      The Strategic Plan explains the anticipated impact of technology; competing priorities, competition, market footprint changes, immediate priorities, organizational developments, values, and guiding principles. It clearly defines the Strategic Business Objectives and provides clear guidance for the development of driving and supporting roadmaps.

   b. Value Proposition and Discipline

      The Strategic Plan provides clear direction on the company Value Proposition and Value Discipline focus. They outline how the company will differentiate as a Class A performer in its chosen markets.

   c. Strategic Business Objectives

      The Strategic Business Objectives are clearly stated and formally agreed. Each is owned by a member of the Leadership Team. The objectives are the driving force for change throughout the organization and used to develop the hierarchy of goals and measures.

   d. Validity and Affordability

      The Strategic Plan has operational analysis and plans to ensure that it is valid and achievable and contains sufficient financial analysis to ensure that it is viable and can be funded, before it is communicated to support the development of roadmaps.

   e. Risk Analysis

      The key risks are formally identified and documented, and formal mitigation plans are developed and deployed as required.

   f. Organizational Roles

      Current and future organizational roles are fully understood and have been communicated throughout the organization.

6. **The Assumptions generated through all parts of the Strategic Planning process are captured and formally documented. They are revalidated as additional information becomes available and are regularly reviewed and monitored.**

   a. Documentation of Assumptions

   The Assumptions made in the construction and the agreement of the Strategic Plan are formally documented and communicated. Ownership of Assumptions is clear, ensuring understanding.

   b. Validity

   The Assumptions are tested to ensure they are valid, confirmed, and applied throughout the business. Wherever possible, they are measured by their owners so that early warning of change is given.

   c. Monitoring and Reporting

   Key Assumptions are monitored and reported through the Integrated Business Planning process regularly.

BRINGING THE FUTURE INTO TODAY

7. **The Strategic Plan is supported by driving roadmaps for the core processes of the business market, product and portfolio, supply chain, and finance. These collectively deliver the company goals and Strategic Business Objectives.**

   a. Critical Success Factors Identified

   Market, Product and Portfolio, and Supply Chain Roadmaps each include identified annual Critical Success Factors that need to be achieved to meet the Strategic Business Objectives.

   b. Market Roadmap

   A Market Roadmap has been developed based on the direction provided by the Strategic Plan. It defines the geography of the business and the market sectors to be pursued. It is designed to meet the growth and profitability aspirations and drives the company Demand Management processes, review, and decision making.

c. Products and Services Roadmap

A Product and Portfolio Roadmap has been developed based on the direction provided by the Strategic Plan and informed by the Market Roadmap. It defines the portfolio of products and services that the company wishes to sell and how that will change over time for each product family or brand. It is designed to meet profit margin aspirations and drives the company Product Management processes, review, and decision making.

d. Supply Chain Roadmap

A Supply Chain Roadmap has been developed based on the direction provided by the Strategic Plan and informed by the Market and Product and Portfolio Roadmaps. It covers processes from suppliers to consumers and from customer orders to invoicing and defines how these will be designed to meet service and cost targets and to introduce new products and services effectively. It defines the role and focus of each Supply Chain and Supply Point and drives the company supply processes, reviews, and decision making.

e. Financial Roadmap

A Financial Roadmap has been developed from the financial views of the other three driving roadmaps. This is used to ensure the driving roadmaps support the Strategic Plan. It confirms the funding for the Strategic Plan, how it will be supported, and how shareholder value and returns will be protected and grown. It defines potential sources of funds and how those funds will be used. It outlines how financial information will be developed to promote and support advances in the business.

8. **Detailed roadmaps for key supporting functions are derived from the Strategic Plan and driving roadmaps and include, as a minimum, People Operations, Information Technology, Quality Assurance, Data, and any other process enablers important to the business.**

a. People Operations Roadmap

The role of people as a major differentiator is understood, and a roadmap exists to focus the acquisition, development, recognition, and motivation of the skills, competencies, and behaviors that are key to delivery of the Strategic Plan and all roadmaps. It includes practical succession planning to cover potential gaps in key positions and competencies.

b. Information Technology Roadmap

A roadmap exists that prioritizes planned investment in Information Technology to support business processes and all roadmaps. It sets out the architecture and framework for systems and communication tools for the future and identifies education and training needs and required behaviors to ensure business gains from Information Technology investments.

c. Quality Assurance Roadmap

A roadmap exists that identifies how Quality Assurance will support all aspects of the business in pursuit of its Strategic Business Objectives.

d. Data Roadmap

A roadmap exists that defines the static and dynamic data needs of the business and its partners and how they will be satisfied. Its implementation is owned by the Leadership Team. Data quality and integrity are understood as foundation requirements and discipline for excellence and are measured throughout.

9. **Multi-year programs, which are used to help define the Business Plan, are structured by fiscal year and focus on providing greater granularity to the driving and supporting roadmaps. They are used throughout the company for team goal setting.**

a. Programs

Using the roadmaps, programs with a multi-year horizon are developed, providing increased granularity of the actions required to achieve the roadmaps. Roadmaps define the yearly targets through Criticial Success Factors that enable clear programs to be defined.

b. Affordability

The resource requirement of the Business Plan is regularly reviewed, and affordability is formally checked to ensure validity.

c. Integrated Business Planning

The Business Plan is the prime reference for Integrated Business Planning.

10. Projects are developed from the programs to determine the actions required in the first year. These are the main drivers of the company's Annual Plan (or Budget), management control, and gap-closing activity.

a. Projects

Projects supporting the multi-year programs are developed and approved for action. Project action plans include the details necessary for resourcing and monitoring quarterly through Key Performance Indicators (KPIs). These project action plans are inputs to the Annual Plan (or Budget), which shows, in depth, an integrated view of how the Strategic Plan will be met.

b. Alignment to Strategy

The projects constituting the Annual Plan are driven top down from the programs supporting the Strategic Plan. They are also monitored and adjusted bottom up through Integrated Business Planning to ensure alignment with the multi-year Business Plan.

STRATEGY DEPLOYMENT

11. The priority of strategic programs and projects is determined through resolution of competing priorities and the Strategic Business Objectives. These priorities determine skill and capability requirements. Programs and projects are justified with unbiased business cases demonstrating a compelling need aligned to strategy and provide a case for change.

a. Performance and Capability Gap Analysis

The gap between current capability and future plans and needs is understood, and the benefits and time phasing of planned changes are quantified.

b. Competing Priorities

Proposed initiatives that compete with each other for attention are assessed using established and agreed criteria and are prioritized to the overall business needs during the horizon of the Strategic Plan.

c. Skill and Competence Analysis

Skills and competencies are formally assessed during Strategic Planning against the strategic plan, roadmaps, programs, and projects. Strengths and weaknesses enable a gap analysis, and improvements are planned. Gap-closure actions are assigned and drive the education, training, selection, and succession plans for the business.

12. Roadmaps are converted into goals at every level of the business with detailed and prioritized action and resource plans. They are cascaded and explained, demonstrating the need and plan for change.

a. Communication Process and Listening

The Vision for the business is widely communicated in a succinct, consistent, and repeatable way with opportunity for comment and feedback. Strategic goals and plans are cascaded to working levels with ownership and sponsorship.

b. Deployment of Goals and Targets

The performance targets required to fulfill the Strategic Plan and the goals outlined in approved and planned programs and projects are represented as goals and targets at all levels of the business. Accountabilities are assigned and are part of the Performance Management process.

c. Detailed Project Plans

Approved programs and projects have detailed plans for goal achievement with supporting resource and capability plans to develop and allocate the appropriate skills and competencies.

d. People Development Plans

Plans are developed and deployed to prepare people for the change program and projects. There is a process in place to identify development needs and potential, and individual personal development plans are instituted. As these evolve, they are used as inputs to development of the People Operations Roadmap.

e. Measure and Review

Formal processes and tools are used to manage, review, and measure programs, projects, and their goals at all levels. Management by exception is commonplace, and proactive corrective action plans are communicated.

EVALUATION AND CONTROL

13. **Formal and informal periodic reviews are held to confirm the alignment of strategies at all company levels and between core processes and specialist support functions.**

    a. Diagnostic Review

    As a minimum annually, a formal Diagnostic Review of strategy deployment is undertaken. This will usually be a complete review of one sample Strategic Business Objective to gauge the depth of its understanding throughout the business and the alignment of all business processes to achieve it. This review will include any challenge to strategic assumptions as identified through Integrated Business Planning.

    b. Reflection

    At least twice per year, the diagnostic is supported by an informal reflection of the Strategic Plan and roadmaps where a few key individuals come together to assess the health and understanding of at least one Strategic Business Objective.

    c. Resource Allocation

    Approved strategic projects are included in the reporting and resource allocations in Integrated Business Planning for programs and projects.

14. **Program and project progress is reviewed through Integrated Business Planning to identify gaps and enable decisions to be made to realign and ensure Critical Success Factors are achieved.**

    a. Program and Project Organization

    An organization exists to manage all strategic programs and projects. It gives visibility of their progress and enables balanced multi-functional priorities and resource allocation.

    b. Project Reviews

    Project plans are regularly reviewed by line managers and sponsors from the Leadership Team, and decisions are made to keep them on course.

c. Results Tracking

Projected and actual business gains are measured, and project-based assumptions are reviewed to ensure that a project remains viable and worthy of completion.

d. Communication

Project launch, progress, and completion are widely communicated to recognize the efforts of those involved and to create an ongoing excitement and appetite for change throughout the organization as well as with Value Chain partners.

BUSINESS STRATEGY MANAGEMENT PROCESS

15. A dynamic process exists to ensure that the impacts of decisions and events on the Strategic Plan and roadmaps are visible, understood, and agreed.

a. Integrated Business Planning

The Integrated Business Planning process reviews the activities and forward plans for all company processes and ensures that their integrated results meet the programs and Business Plan.

b. Short-Term Decisions and Long-Term Alignment

Integrated Business Planning ensures that day-to-day events and decisions are fully aligned to longer-term plans for the business. If not fully aligned, business gaps are made visible for determination of gap-closing decisions and actions.

RISK MANAGEMENT

16. The Strategic Plan and roadmaps are systematically and rigorously analyzed for risk. Contingency plans exist to mitigate identified risks.

a. Risk Analysis

A standard method of risk analysis, which identifies comparative criticality of risks, has been adopted and is widely used at all levels of the business on an ongoing basis.

b. Risk Management

   Plans and actions exist and are updated to eliminate risk or to reduce it to manageable levels.

c. Contingency Planning

   Contingency plans exist at all levels of the business to minimize the impact of known risks and to shorten disruption and recovery time.

PERFORMANCE MEASUREMENT

17. **A hierarchy of balanced measures is used to assess and drive company performance to achieve its Strategic Business Objectives and Vision.**

   a. Integrated Measures

      A balanced suite of measures is in place at the top of the company, identifying how the interests of all the stakeholders are managed. This suite is at the top of a measurement hierarchy for the whole business that is used to monitor progress and drive action.

   b. Visibility

      The measures for individuals or a team are succinctly summarized and show trends as well as spot performance. Measures are clearly displayed for everyone to see and are designed to encourage improvement.

18. **Measures are hierarchically structured and integrated so that the impact of performance on the business is clearly visible and understood. Measures at all levels can be linked back to the Critical Success Factors and, hence, the Strategic Business Objectives.**

   a. Team Targets

      Company-wide measures are cascaded through all levels so that each person or team clearly understands their targets and performance expectations, including how they relate to overall company performance in pursuit of Strategic Business Objectives.

   b. Driving Improvement

      Measures are used to drive performance improvement and to encourage Continuous Improvement by individuals and teams.

c. Relevance

All measures can be linked back to Critical Success Factors as defined in the roadmaps. They measure business performance and/or process performance in pursuit of Strategic Business Objectives.

BEHAVIORS AND COMPETENCIES

19. **The Strategic Planning process is supported by both cultural and behavioral development, which ensures positive team ownership of the entire plan, with strong leadership and individual accountabilities.**

a. Leadership and Excitement

Strategic Planning is led by the Chief Executive Officer and the Leadership Team and utilizes a process to engage more people, from all levels, as the Strategic Plan, roadmaps, programs, and projects are developed. When deployed, it must excite and engage its stakeholders.

b. Ownership

Performance, programs, projects, and actions are owned at the appropriate level and are sponsored within the Leadership Team.

c. Communication

Formal communication is used to progressively cascade the Strategic Plan and roadmaps throughout the business and engage the workforce. It is actively reinforced through everyday, informal communication.

d. Demonstrated Leadership

Leadership demonstrates a disciplined use of the deployed strategy in its decision making and company-wide communications to keep the strategy alive at all levels.

20. **Competencies: unique skills, talents, and proficiencies ensure individual, team, and business success.**

a. Leadership

They have the ability to create the big picture and engage the organization with the vision.

b. <u>Strategy Development</u>

Strategy Development enables the ability to synthesize global perspectives, the geopolitical environment, and economic and macro market conditions.

c. <u>Strategy Deployment</u>

This is the capability to develop a coherent plan and supporting organizational design to successfully communicate and action the Strategy throughout.

2
MANAGING AND LEADING PEOPLE

PURPOSE

To ensure a Leadership and Team Based Culture exists to capitalize on agile organizational changes in alignment to changing market and customer dynamics. To develop the capabilities and competencies required to optimize plans through the development of analytics and drive the business to Class A levels of performance.

POSITIONING

Managing and Leading People includes all aspects of People Operations from Strategic Planning to establishing a team-based environment to support Business Excellence and Class A levels of performance. It includes Knowledge Management, analytics, education, training, innovation, organization design, leadership style, teamwork, empowerment, appraisals, mentoring, measurement, communication, health, safety, the environment, transformation, and decision making. The chapter supports all processes of the business and ensures the leadership and people needs are identified and deployed to support and drive roadmaps.

Process maturity improves over time through education, committed leadership, expert guidance, and focused effort to attain key business milestones.

Done well, a Class A Milestone is achieved at the top of Phase 1 of Business Maturity (see Foundation, Figure I.1). At this stage, good functional team working has been established with two-way communication. Soft management techniques are being used to complement the hard. Trust, honesty, openness, and humor lubricate the organization.

From this Class A Milestone vantage point, we introduce the next level of maturity in the seventh edition of *The Oliver Wight Class A Standard for Business Excellence*.

CHAPTER CONTENT

Driven by Strategy

Integration

Leadership

People in Teams

Talent Development and People Retention

Communication

Organization Design Development and Planning

Business Improvement and Learning

Consistent Working Practices

Management of Health, Safety, Environment, and Community Relations

Performance Measurement

DRIVEN BY STRATEGY

1. The Value Statement and Guiding Principles identify how the company culture will be lived. They are evidenced in all roadmaps and govern behaviors.

a. Values and Guiding Principles Documented and Visible

The Values and Guiding Principles are both documented and visible for all employees. They are well publicized throughout the company. This is a proactive process that seeks to refresh the presentation regularly to ensure their ongoing use.

b. Live Them

Leadership lives the Values and Guiding Principles by best role model behavior. Similar demonstrations from managers, supervisors, team leaders, and all employees are evident.

c. Culture Aligned to Values and Guiding Principles

The Values are the glue that binds the organization together, and the culture is continuously checked for alignment with the Values. The employee engagement survey is part of this process.

d. Linkage to Company Roadmaps

The Value Statements and Guiding Principles can be seen throughout the company's roadmaps as a thread linking them together. The owners can articulate that linkage.

e. Trust

Trust is highly valued throughout the organization. Key behaviors are widely recognized as there is a broad appreciation of the trust equation.

INTEGRATION

2. The People Operations Roadmap is integrated with the driving and supporting roadmaps and demonstrates the commitment to aligning all employees with the Strategic Plan.

a. Create and Document

The People Operations Roadmap is drawn up and owned by the Leadership Team. It is documented and reviewed at least annually to ensure it remains aligned to the driving roadmaps.

b. <u>Integrated and Aligned</u>

The People Operations Roadmap is aligned and integrated with all roadmaps and drives the development of a team-based organization.

c. <u>Awareness</u>

Leadership formally and informally receives feedback from all employees on both the relevance and effectiveness of the People Operations Roadmap. Employee engagement surveys are conducted annually; outcomes and actions are recommunicated to all.

d. <u>Coordination</u>

People Operations activities are coordinated via the Integrated Business Planning process to ensure alignment with all other plans.

LEADERSHIP

3. The Leadership Team articulate and demonstrate leadership, individually and collectively. They are widely recognized as a team.

a. <u>Understanding of Leadership versus Management</u>

The Leadership Team know and understand leadership qualities. They can demonstrate the difference and balance between management and leadership through a shared understanding and application of Situational Leadership.

b. <u>Demonstration Role Model</u>

The Leadership Team, individually and collectively, are seen by the rest of the organization as role models for leadership. They constantly drive the organization to improve, and set and live up to high business standards.

c. <u>Leadership Capabilities for the Future</u>

The Leadership Team recognize that leadership styles, skills, and abilities will change over time. Plans are in place to ensure the right mix for future team requirements.

4. Leadership is encouraged and rewarded throughout the organization.

a. <u>Identification of Leaders</u>

Employees at all levels of the organization who demonstrate leadership qualities are empowered to take on challenging assignments.

b. <u>Education and Training</u>

Employees with leadership potential are educated and trained to nurture the required future skills and behaviors.

c. <u>Encouragement, Reward, Recognition, and Visibility</u>

Employees who demonstrate and meet leadership challenges receive appropriate recognition and rewards. Successes are celebrated and made visible to all.

d. <u>Leadership Culture</u>

The culture supports the development of potential future leaders. Mentors are assigned. Mutual trust and accountability are visible. Mistakes made while learning are tolerated. The rules are clear, and credit is shared.

PEOPLE IN TEAMS

5. Teams are utilized as the primary means to direct, organize, and carry out work.

a. <u>Team Selection and Charter</u>

Consistent criteria are used to select team members. Teams develop and work to an agreed charter to satisfy the scope of their tasks.

b. <u>Team Training and Team Building</u>

Teamwork is sustained using training and team-building activities.

c. <u>Team Performance, Results, and Recognition</u>

The company rewards team performance, not just that of individuals. Team results are maintained and displayed by the team.

d. <u>Teams Aligned to Business Processes</u>

Teams enable business processes that drive business goals before functional or personal needs.

6. An empowerment culture exists to support decision making and enable teams and employees to achieve their goals and responsibilities.

a. <u>Team Based</u>

When selected for teams, people understand their roles, their responsibilities, and the scope of their empowerment.

b. Empowerment Increases with Maturity

As the company's environment matures toward self-managed teams, a boundary-less mind-set develops, increasing the effectiveness of empowerment.

c. People Accept Empowerment and Are Accountable for their Actions

People openly and readily state their accountabilities and responsibilities. The environment supports learning which is naturally shared team to team. Individuals recognize and embrace their team roles.

TALENT DEVELOPMENT AND PEOPLE RETENTION

7. The development of the people is strategically important and actively deployed, building a database to support the development and retention of people.

a. Resources Fully Committed

The company commits resources, time, and finances to drive talent, skills, and knowledge.

b. Development Planning and Measurement of Success

Education and training are aligned with the Strategic Plan to ensure the right education and training are done and that they are cost-effective. Education and training include the principles of process and behavior change in an organization rather than just fact transfer tied to specific technology.

c. Performance Appraisal (Individual and Team)

Performance appraisals provide employee and team feedback on key performance indicators that are linked to the roadmaps, programs, projects, business processes, and goals. The performance appraisal process includes individual goal setting and personal development plans. They ensure the application of talent, skills, and knowledge gained. The process can provide 360-degree feedback at all levels.

d. Equal Opportunities for Personal Growth

The company maintains the opportunity for advancement of all individuals within the organization equally with other applicants, both inside and outside the company.

8. The People Operations Roadmap assures the talent, competencies, and skills required for the future.

    a. <u>Talent, Competencies, and Skills Defined and Linked to Roles</u>

        Talent, competencies, and skills that are critical to successfully implement the Strategic Plan have been identified in each business process. These talents, competencies, and skills may vary but should include satisfying customer requirements, process knowledge, teamwork, innovation, mentoring, financial competency, analytics, modeling, and governance.

    b. <u>Succession Planning</u>

        Career paths are clearly identified and communicated. Succession planning includes external recruitment. Measures are in place to monitor and improve the deployment of succession plans.

    c. <u>Improving the Employee Life Cycle</u>

        There is an established process to improve the Employee Life Cycle, focusing on every part, from recruitment and selection to career development, coaching, mentoring, and retention.

    d. <u>Developing and Retaining the Right People</u>

        The People Operations Roadmap ensures that the Employee Life Cycle takes into account all needs, both team and individual, to ensure employees fully value the benefits of expanding their contributions and actively extending their life in the organization. Employees own their personal development with funding available through the roadmap.

    e. <u>Employee Departures Used to Improve Talent Management</u>

        Regretful employee departures are viewed as process failures and as opportunities to improve Talent Management.

COMMUNICATION

9. Good communication is up and down the organization and between all functions, driving and supporting business processes.

    a. <u>Natural Communication</u>

        The organization encourages natural communication between people. People at every level automatically give and look to receive information to help them in their jobs.

b. Communication Etiquette

   The organization has educated people at all levels on how to communicate effectively. These skills are two-way, and positive communication behaviors are required from all employees.

c. Meeting Skills and Behaviors

   There is a focus on the importance of meeting skills and behaviors. Training has been given. Positive meeting skills and behaviors are consistently reinforced.

10. The company has an effective Communications Framework.

a. Definition

   There is a comprehensive Communications Framework laying out the frequency, content, purpose, level of detail, venues, and importance of listening skills, for communication in the organization. Communication covers all levels and it is regularly audited for structure and effectiveness.

b. Closed-Loop Feedback (Perception Is Reality)

   The communication process actively seeks feedback from employees at all levels. There is recognition that perception of the message is reality.

c. Face-to-Face Team Briefs

   Face-to-face team briefing is practiced monthly throughout the organization and cascades through all levels with feedback of all answered questions to all.

ORGANIZATION DESIGN DEVELOPMENT AND PLANNING

11. The organization is planned and designed to ensure achievement of Strategic Business Objectives.

a. Alignment with Strategy

   The organization is aligned with the Strategic Plan such that the organization is optimally structured and staffed.

b. Simplification and Adaptability

The levels in the organization structure have been minimized. The organization is flexible and adaptable to changing business conditions.

c. Balancing Function and Process

The organization balances function and process. Functional depth is provided while recognizing business process characteristics. Business Excellence is fostered by design to meet internal and external customer needs.

d. Effective Planning

The company adapts the organization with an agile capability in response to changes in the market and customers. The expectations for roles, tasks, and business objectives are concurrently aligned.

e. Compensation

Compensation structure attracts and retains competent employees. Team-based rewards are important.

12. Employee policies and procedures are consistent with the organizational design and plans. They reflect a thought-through approach for employees and are seen to be followed.

a. People Operations Procedures

People Operations policies and procedures are available and are reviewed at least annually. Important policies and procedures are visibly posted in the workplace.

b. Staffing and Resource Planning

Staffing and resource planning, including the use of temporary workers and outsourcing as well as selection and redeployment, are driven by the Strategic Plan and People Operations Roadmap.

c. Employee Relations and Recognition

Excellent employee relations are established, and leadership actions reinforce this. Recognition of individuals and teams is widespread.

d. Employee Welfare and Quality of Life

The company concerns itself with quality of life and the welfare of employees, actively improving the human side of work. The need for work–life balance is considered in job design.

BUSINESS IMPROVEMENT AND LEARNING

13. The management of change is an ongoing requirement and is a way of life for the entire organization.

    a. Education

        Leadership and management embrace change and demonstrate this to all through the application of resources to business improvement.

    b. Advocates and Change Agents

        Advocates and change agents ensure that individuals and teams provide a welcoming atmosphere for new ideas and implement business improvement projects supported by their behaviors and actions.

    c. Implementation

        Change is planned and managed effectively, using proven methodologies.

14. A learning organization has been established with active education and training reflecting current and future business needs.

    a. The Need for Continuous Learning

        In an environment of dynamic change, continuous shared learning and the application of shared knowledge support business improvement.

    b. Knowledge Management

        Knowledge is captured and built into processes and procedures. There is a routine capture and retention of comprehensive knowledge about the business.

    c. Learning Benefits Individual Employees and the Organization

        Employee development emphasizes learning that increases employee competencies and creative potential to support innovation and analytics.

CONSISTENT WORKING PRACTICES

15. Policies, procedures, and practices are applied consistently and effectively.

    a. Formal and Visible

        Policies, procedures, and work practices are documented and visible throughout.

b. Educated and Owned

   All employees own the working practices that apply to them.

c. Traceable and Auditable

   In line with best practices, all policies, procedures, and practices are easily traceable and auditable by internal or external auditors.

d. Compliant with Widely Recognized Standards

   Policies, procedures, and practices are universally compliant with applicable standards recognized to apply to their business.

MANAGEMENT OF HEALTH, SAFETY, ENVIRONMENT, AND COMMUNITY RELATIONS

16. Managing safety, health, and the environment is embraced throughout.

a. People

   Employees view their own, their colleagues', and visitors' safety as their number one priority. The company understands the people and business benefits of a healthy workforce and supports employee well-being. Safety, health, and environmental awareness education and training are ongoing requirements for all and are part of the induction program.

b. Compliance with Regulation and Legislation

   Current health, safety, and environmental regulations and legislative requirements are fully applied. Any changes are communicated promptly, and employees are educated and trained accordingly.

c. Tools, Auditing, and Measurement

   All employees have sufficient knowledge and the proper materials and equipment to do their jobs safely and with minimum impact on the environment. Performance measures are included in the portfolio of key business measures for the company. Regular audits are conducted in the workplace.

d. Continuous Improvement and Elimination of Failure and Waste

   All employees are committed to reducing the company's impact on the environment through the promotion of best practices and the continuous elimination of failure and waste. Opportunities for process improvements, recycling, and the reduction of waste output are constantly being identified and implemented.

e. <u>Prevention</u>

The company recognizes the importance of prevention in terms of health, safety, and environmental problems.

17. The company demonstrates a continuous, positive commitment to the local community.

a. <u>Proactive Commitment to Community Relations</u>

There is a demonstrable, proactive commitment from the Leadership Team to strengthen relations with the local community. Continuous efforts are made to earn the trust and goodwill of the community. Two-way communication with the community is in place.

b. <u>Community Validation</u>

The company is respected by the local community. The benefits the company brings to the community are recognized. The company is a good neighbor.

c. <u>Leadership</u>

Leadership ensures that everyone in the organization understands the importance and value of good community relations.

d. <u>Wide Range of Community Activities</u>

There is widespread employee involvement in communications and activities with the local community.

e. <u>Integration of Business Activity and Community Activity</u>

Where possible, business activities are supportive of community needs, and community issues are considered part of the strategic and tactical implementation plans.

PERFORMANCE MEASUREMENT

18. There is a balanced hierarchy of people measures that are fair and effective. They support the cultural environment for Business Excellence. Measures are integrated as part of a Business Scorecard.

a. <u>Business Excellence</u>

A balance of people measures is designed to support Business Excellence and is integrated with Strategic Business Objectives by a Measurement Hierarchy.

b. Reviewed

The key measures are regularly reviewed to align People Management activities to the People Operations Roadmap and achievement of Critical Success Factors. Key Performance Indicators and targets are changed to maintain visibility and prioritize improvement.

c. Hierarchical Linkage

There is a clear hierarchical link between the suite of key measures for each business process and the Business Scorecard. Once process proficiency has been established, the measures will be delegated or redefined or the targets revised.

d. Competitive Advantage

Key measures and associated Key Performance Indicators are a competitive advantage rather than a goal and drive individual and team-based behaviors.

e. Natural Feedback Mechanisms

Giving and receiving feedback has become natural. Feedback mechanisms and tools, such as surveys, social media, and virtual interaction, in addition to face-to-face interaction, are used to gain information to gauge employee satisfaction and organizational climate.

f. Measured Results Are Acted Upon

Leadership owns the analyzed gaps between desired and actual performance in all areas. The measure demonstrates business improvement and are benchmarked against Class A Business Excellence.

19. **Process measures are used to ensure effective and efficient People Management activities. Performance is monitored relative to established targets, and corrective action is taken to close gaps.**

a. Recruiting and Retention

The cost of employee acquisition is monitored and continuously optimized. Employee retention measures, such as service longevity and turnover, are used to manage the workforce effectively.

b. Employee Development

Education and training spending per employee is linked to business improvement and Business Excellence measures.

c. <u>High-Performance Work Environment</u>

Team and individual results are measured versus required deliverables. Reliability and time to delivery are improving.

20. Business performance measures are used to ensure efficient People Management activities. Performance is monitored relative to established targets, and corrective action is taken to close gaps.

a. <u>Education and Training</u>

Education and training spending per employee is linked to business improvement and Business Excellence measures.

b. <u>Training Programs Strategically Focused</u>

Training programs are used to develop skills required to deliver results effectively in support of strategy and appropriate roadmaps.

c. <u>Capability Development Consistent with Roadmaps</u>

Capabilities and associated competencies required to deliver the strategy are actively developed. Measures are in place to help assess organizational capability and individual competency gaps and effectiveness of resulting development initiatives.

3
DRIVING BUSINESS IMPROVEMENT

PURPOSE

To deploy a comprehensive Business Improvement approach utilizing a full suite of improvement methods to drive business results to Class A performance. The approach is deployed in support of behavior change and recognizes the hierarchy of process, the hierarchy of performance measurement, and their ownership.

POSITIONING

Business Improvement, aligned to business maturity, includes all recognized methodologies appropriately structured and deployed to drive sustainable performance improvement, drive behavior change, and secure world-class business performance. The approach enables the application of Continuous Improvement tools, Lean methodology, and Six Sigma and the utilization of an Agile capability to manage unforeseen business and short-term opportunities. Ownership of the methods has been established, enabled through education, and their use is guided by a clear understanding of the Strategic Plan.

The sequence of this chapter follows the maturity journey; early improvement techniques are addressed in the opening definitions building to more mature techniques later in the chapter.

Class A Business Improvement is the successful and sustainable improvement of process and business performance through their broad application throughout the organization. The elimination of failure and waste and the resulting process velocity across all business processes support cost-effective Agility.

CHAPTER CONTENT

Driven by Strategy

Integration

Insights

Ownership and Involvement

Continuous Improvement

Velocity throughout Business Processes

Responsiveness to Customer

Process Variation

Knowledge Capture and Management

Asset Management

Business Transformation and Innovation

Behaviors and Competencies

Performance Measurement

DRIVEN BY STRATEGY

1. **The Strategic Plan has been expanded to include a series of driving and supporting roadmaps. These roadmaps direct the improvement activities, their interrelationship, their timing, and their expected contribution to Business Excellence.**

   a. <u>Programs and Projects</u>

   Programs and projects have been prioritized based on the Strategic Plan and roadmaps. These are used to develop and deploy required competencies, improvement tools, and techniques.

   b. <u>Ownership and Resource Assignment</u>

   Ownership of the Business Improvement Roadmap, programs, and projects has been defined, and resources have been assigned.

   c. <u>Review of Progress</u>

   The Leadership Team reviews progress against the Business Improvement Roadmap regularly. The review includes progress in terms of programs, projects, timing, resource requirements, budget, and benefits realization.

INTEGRATION

2. **Business Improvement activities are coordinated through Integrated Business Planning. Employees can relate improvement programs and projects that they are involved in to the company's Vision, Mission, Strategic Plan, and Roadmaps.**

   a. <u>Integration</u>

   All improvement plans are reviewed through Integrated Business Planning. All known resource requirements and expected benefits are included in the current Integrated Business Plan.

   b. <u>Communication on Progress</u>

   Visible performance measures are used to maintain awareness of Business Improvement activities and progress toward the Strategic Business Objectives.

c. Employee Understanding

Employees understand how their specific improvement programs and projects contribute to the vision, strategic business objectives, value proposition, competitive priorities, and roadmaps of the business. This clarifies their individual roles and contributions to the realization of the Strategic Plan and Business Improvement objectives.

INSIGHTS

3. **Ongoing competitor analysis is continuously assessed to ensure a competitive advantage is maintained. Performance levels are established, and the business is focused on attaining sustainable Class A levels of performance.**

a. Driving and Supporting Business Processes

The driving and supporting business processes have been determined and defined. Their relative contributions and relationships to overall business performance and the competitive priorities are understood. Process owners drive their performance to Class A levels.

b. Class A Performance

Class A performance has been researched and defined in terms of both business sector and business processes. This information has been used to set internal goals and define Key Performance Indicators.

c. Competitor Analysis

Formal analysis of competitor capability and performance levels is conducted regularly. This information is used to identify competitive opportunities, which are integrated into the Business Improvement priorities.

d. Strategic Business Objectives

The Strategic Plan and Strategic Business Objectives are deployed and owned.

4. **Benchmarking is carried out across business processes. Process owners use this knowledge to drive Business Improvement.**

a. Benchmarking

Benchmarking activities are routinely undertaken; process performances are benchmarked against best-known performers internally and from all sectors externally.

b. Sharing and Sustaining

   There is a formal process for implementing, sharing, and sustaining best practices within the business. The knowledge obtained is stored and readily accessible.

c. External Business Critiques

   External visits, assessments, and audits are used to identify and understand best practices to enhance existing Business Improvement plans.

d. Business Excellence and World-Class Performance

   An understanding of Business Excellence and World-Class Performance is maintained via education, academic references or papers, and relevant associations. This knowledge is used to drive internal targets higher.

OWNERSHIP AND INVOLVEMENT

5. **Ownership of and accountability for process, data, information, and assets are assigned to people and teams for maintenance and improvement.**

a. Improvement Agenda

   There is widespread appreciation for Business Improvement, and employee teams can articulate the need for ongoing improvements.

b. Team Ownership Naturally Assumed

   Teams take ownership of their working environment. They visually display clear expectations and present their shared and ongoing achievements.

c. Team Ownership

   Team-based ownership of the working environment and improvement activities exists, and processes have been reorganized to enable colocation of the team.

6. **Ownership and accountability are clear and drive Business Improvement.**

a. Business Improvement Ideas

   Time is regularly allocated for teams to analyze future business requirements and develop ideas to ensure the success of strategic roadmaps.

b. Visibility of Program and Project Ownership

A comprehensive structure of improvement activities is in place, maintained, and communicated. This provides visibility of both ownership and the level of involvement in Business Improvement initiatives.

c. Team Ownership

Teams implement all appropriate Business Improvement initiatives to align with business goals and timescales.

CONTINUOUS IMPROVEMENT

7. There is a culture of Continuous Improvement.

a. Company-wide Involvement

All employees actively drive Business Improvement activities individually and as part of a team.

b. Strategic Alignment

All initiatives demonstrate a clear relationship and expected contribution to the Strategic and Business Plans.

c. Customer Value

The value anticipated by the customers is known throughout the organization, and Continuous Improvement is aligned to systematically deliver this understanding.

d. Teams

Teams are the organization's norm.

e. Empowerment

Teams understand their level of authority and know at what point to seek management involvement or authorization.

f. Visual Management

Visual management techniques are deployed at all levels in the organization.

8. An improvement framework guides Business Improvement.

a. Structured Communication

Standard templates are used to capture and communicate Business Improvement projects throughout the organization along with the realized benefits.

b. Collaborative Partnerships

Partnerships have been formally established and are used to drive mutual Business Improvement projects and benefits. All Business Improvement initiatives are communicated through shared measures and are used to signal successful completion and ongoing maintenance of the new standards.

VELOCITY THROUGHOUT BUSINESS PROCESSES

9. The business deploys Lean as a means of delivering customer value, attaining Class A levels of process Velocity to support Agility.

a. Value Chain

Consumer and customer value has been systematically communicated through the business and Supply Chain. Each Supply Chain Node can determine its delivery response in accordance with this understanding.

b. Value Stream Mapping

Value Stream Mapping is used to determine where waste can be eliminated to drive velocity improvements and reduce costs. Elimination of waste and velocity improvement of all core processes are measured and tracked to demonstrate improvement.

c. Velocity

Class A Velocity has been determined, and core process teams set improvement objectives accordingly.

d. Lean Deployment

Lean principles are shared throughout the organization, and this common knowledge is used to enable a cost-effective response to business needs, internally and externally, through the systematic reduction of the 11 types of waste such as the waste of overproduction, unnecessary motion, and of defects.

10. The concept of pull has been understood and appropriately applied when necessary in the business.

a. Pull from Customer Demand

Pull from customer demand is a competitive advantage and is a means of contributing to the Value Proposition. This understanding has been effectively applied and the resultant benefits realized.

b. Kanban

Techniques such as Kanban are used to drive replenishment in processes where appropriate. Where Kanban is used, people can articulate calculation methods and understand that the Kanban quantity is itself waste and, hence, a further opportunity for improvement. Where Kanban is used, its rules are defined and all violations measured.

c. Planning

Planners understand and can articulate the approach and procedures for pull from customer demand and apply this understanding when needed.

RESPONSIVENESS TO CUSTOMER

11. The business has a competitive advantage, from rapid and cost-effective responses to customer requirements, from flexible and Agile processes and teams.

a. Agility

Planned and cost-effective Agility is enabled throughout the organization, delivering the promised responsiveness.

b. Systematic Agile Business Improvement

Systematically, improvement projects increase flexibility and the business's ability to effectively respond to change.

c. Supply Chain

Business Agility is also applied throughout the Supply Chain, extending the involvement to include customers and suppliers.

12. **The business has the Agility to reconfigure its organization and processes. Through modeling and analytics, this reconfiguration is done to stimulate or respond to changes in the marketplace to secure improved competitive advantage.**

    a. Modeling and Analytics

    Scenarios and analytics are used to support a system-based modeling capability to identify further business and Supply Chain recommendations to be evaluated through Integrated Business Planning.

    b. Business, Product, and Service Agility

    Planned Agility enables a cost-effective response to unforeseen marketplace opportunities or changes to immediate customer needs with the supply of product or services but, at the same time, delivering published plans.

PROCESS VARIATION

13. **Formal processes to reduce variation are applied throughout the business using analytics and optimization tools that drive Business Improvement beyond what the human can manage.**

    a. Measurement

    Business and process-based measurements are in place. Measures are used to provide feedback on performance and to drive improvement through the reduction of variation.

    b. Variation

    Process variation is measured and is continuously being reduced. Statistical problem-solving techniques are deployed to reduce variation of activities toward Six Sigma levels of performance.

    c. Statistical Process Control

    Process control and consistency are fundamental to quality and performance improvement. Statistical process control is understood and used throughout the business to maintain control and prevent process failure.

    d. Root-Cause Analysis

    Root-Cause Analysis and associated tools and techniques are used extensively throughout the business. The causes of failure and deviation are routinely identified, and Root-Cause Analysis is used to determine and implement permanent corrective action.

KNOWLEDGE CAPTURE AND MANAGEMENT

14. Knowledge and learning are formally captured and integrated into business processes. The evolving knowledge database enables an analytics capability.

a. Knowledge Capture

A process exists to capture and disseminate knowledge. This process is owned and reviewed to ensure effectiveness. Knowledge is captured from both success and failure. All knowledge obtained is stored in the appropriate areas of the business's knowledge database.

b. Sharing Learning

Learning from Business Improvement activities is captured and naturally shared. This sharing and capturing of knowledge enable the development of an analytics capability.

c. Education

Employees are encouraged to attend relevant educational courses and external events. The importance of sharing and applying the learning from such activities is understood.

d. Knowledge Availability

To gain knowledge from customers, suppliers, consumers, competitors, the Internet, the media, TV, books, white papers, universities, and other bodies of knowledge is recognized as essential. However, the knowledge acquired must be common, shared, and applied through teams to ensure employees, at all levels, share the same understanding and use.

e. Benchmarking

Benchmarking, internally and externally, is routinely done to formally identify and share knowledge, capabilities, and applications.

15. Employees at all levels willingly transfer their knowledge into business processes and system databases, enabling analytics.

   a. <u>Knowledge Sharing and Capture</u>

     Knowledge is recognized as a competitive advantage, which is widely understood and accepted. People actively capture knowledge and transfer it into processes and systems.

   b. <u>Analytics and Business Data</u>

     The business and organization apply analytics to business data to describe, predict, and improve business performance. Areas within analytics include, for example: predictive analytics, prescriptive analytics, business decision making, inventory optimization, marketing optimization and marketing mix modeling, price, and promotion modeling.

ASSET MANAGEMENT

16. There is a formal management process in place to control and protect all business equipment.

   a. <u>Equipment Ownership</u>

     Ownership of business equipment is clearly defined. The owners proactively assure the condition, performance, and improvement of their equipment.

   b. <u>Asset Control</u>

     All business equipment is subject to regular auditing to confirm existence, operational status, and inclusion in financial records.

   c. <u>Planned Maintenance</u>

     A Planned Maintenance Program with an 18- to 24-month horizon is in place for all productive equipment and plants, based on demonstrated, preventative, and predicted data. Adherence to the Planned Maintenance Program is measured and routinely reviewed. Planned Maintenance activity is related to equipment reliability on an ongoing basis. The relationship is used to determine future maintenance plans.

d. Business Systems

Performance of the Business Systems is monitored, and findings are routinely reviewed for action.

e. Total Productive Maintenance

Key equipment is subject to Total Productive Maintenance. All relevant employees are involved, and training programs exist to develop the associated skills and competencies. Overall equipment effectiveness is measured and improved.

f. Reliability-Centered Maintenance

"Mean time between failure" and "mean time to recover" are key business performance measures. Technical maintenance activities are prioritized using these measures. An associated improvement plan is in place, and Continuous Improvement in both areas can be demonstrated. The Maintenance Team, in accordance with the stated equipment reliability, manages inventory of critical spares.

BUSINESS TRANSFORMATION AND INNOVATION

17. **Business Transformation Programs to drive step-change improvement are proactively identified through innovative thinking and execution.**

a. Strategic Alignment of Innovation

The Leadership Team proactively identifies transformational opportunities that support the Strategic Plan of the business. The Leadership Team recognizes the importance of idea generation and resulting innovation and enables resources for this purpose.

b. Ideas and Innovation Analysis

A formal process ensures emphasis, and time is allocated to identification and evaluation of relevant transformational opportunities. Risk mitigation is used to protect those that may fail.

c. Evaluation Process

A formal process for evaluating, selecting, and prioritizing potential ideas and their impact on the Strategic Plan is in place.

d. Implementation and Progress

An implementation methodology is in place that drives successful implementation of Business Transformation. Progress is reviewed through Integrated Business Planning.

e. Third Parties

Third parties are used to critique improvement programs and provide an external contribution to business process idea generation and innovation.

f. Involvement

All areas of the business are encouraged to contribute to step-change improvement through innovative thinking.

BEHAVIORS AND COMPETENCIES

18. There is a commitment to Business Excellence and a passion for sustainable Business Improvement.

a. Leadership for Continuous Improvement

The Leadership Team is fully supportive of Continuous Improvement activities.

b. Knowledge-Based Decisions

Decisions are based on the availability of knowledge derived from Business Scorecards, data warehouses, and modeling that uses analytics.

c. Ambition

Leadership continuously articulates an ambition to be the best within its chosen proposition. Milestones are used to stage the journey, and everyone understands the need for Business Excellence. Leadership is continuously seeking new opportunities to set higher targets and goals. Continuous Improvement and Business Transformation activities are routinely deployed throughout.

d. Learning Environment

Management seeks opportunities to learn new tools and techniques; ideas are reviewed and trialed. Learning from others is a strength.

e. Process Knowledge

Business process knowledge is essential. The teams, which may include suppliers and customers, work together to transfer knowledge and understanding for improvement.

f. Research and Experimentation

Resource investment for both external and internal research and experimentation activities is made available on an ongoing basis. Investment in research is aligned to competitive priorities and the Strategic Plan.

g. Rewards and Recognition

Individuals and teams are recognized for their contribution, and team success has become the focus.

h. Ownership and Accountability

Individuals and teams have the confidence to make decisions and are held accountable. Potential failure is mitigated through self-managed team ownership. Sponsorship is demonstrated by the Leadership Team.

i. Communication

Communication is a priority, is continuous, is reinforced, and is appropriate to the target audience to ensure company-wide understanding.

j. Decisiveness

In the face of uncertainty, decision making is accelerated because of clear lines of authority.

19. **Competencies; unique skills, talents, and proficiencies ensure individual, team, and business success.**

a. Leadership

There is effective application of Change Management skills.

b. Facilitation and Deployment

There is clarity about Continuous Improvement tools and techniques, their application, and their value to the organization. This should include competency in problem solving, lean/systemic thinking, process thinking, analytical skills, and structured communicating.

PERFORMANCE MEASUREMENT

20. A balanced Measurement Hierarchy defines the link of Strategic Business Objectives to the Business Scorecard and core process measures.

a. Structure

Measures are integrated, are consistent, and drive business performance to deliver the Vision, Mission, and Strategic Plan. Measures are reviewed for relevance, accuracy, tolerances, and targets as performance improves.

b. Balanced View

The Business Scorecard contains extracts from the Measurement Hierarchy that enable a balanced view of business performance.

c. Hierarchy

A Measurement Hierarchy is used to show the linkage of measures from the top to the bottom of the business. The hierarchy has been communicated and is widely understood throughout.

d. Key Performance Indicators Understood

Key Performance Indicators are clearly understood, as *key* defines it as an important measure, *performance* equals a formula to measure performance, and *indicator* defines the current performance against the target that the Key Performance Indicator is focused on achieving.

21. Process measures are included in the Business Scorecard to drive improvement of core business processes and supporting activities.

a. Velocity Ratio

Velocity Ratio is used as a key measure for all core business processes. The company has a stated objective to increase core process velocity.

b. Agility

Process responsiveness is measured and improved for those processes or activities where process Agility is required as a competitive priority.

c. Process Improvement Activity

The number of improvement ideas being both generated and implemented is being continuously measured and is consistent with objectives.

22. Business performance measures are included in the Business Scorecard to drive performance improvement, support business decisions, and set priorities.

a. Cost Benefits

The impact of improvements is reflected and monitored in terms of cost benefits. Optimizing value-added activities is providing simultaneous benefits from growth, productivity, cash, and margin.

b. Added Value

Added Value is being measured on an ongoing basis and shows an improving trend.

c. Improvement Efforts Deliver Results with Increasing Reliability

Measures such as plan attainment, assumptions accuracy, Demand Planning, product/service development, Supply Planning, and inventory optimization are actively used by the appropriate part(s) of the organization to drive improved results.

4

INTEGRATED BUSINESS PLANNING

PURPOSE

To integrate all plans, deploy the business strategy and drive proactive business management. In response to external and internal insights and change, the process uses modeling of scenarios to optimize business plans and performance. The process is enabled by technology to become the driver of Enterprise Integrated Business Planning (EIBP).

POSITIONING

Process maturity improves over time through education, committed leadership, expert guidance, and a focused effort to attain key business milestones.

After embarking on the path to improvement, accountabilities are assigned, the process elements, supporting measures and cadence of the process are implemented. Together, with structured continuous improvement, they drive process transformation.

Done well, a Class A Milestone is achieved at the top of Phase 1 of Business Maturity (see Foundation, Figure I.1). At this stage, the Leadership Team uses the process as the way to run the business. Integrated Business Planning (IBP) becomes the business decision-making process, enabled by risk analysis and what-if scenario planning. It continuously realigns plans for product, demand, supply, and financial projections to support the business strategy. The Annual Business Plan is directly derived from the IBP process, the bottom-up plans are continuously reconciled to the Annual Plan, and Strategic Plan and gaps are managed. The Leadership Team hold themselves accountable and allocate critical resources to most effectively satisfy customers profitably.

From this Class A Milestone vantage point, we introduce this next level of maturity in the seventh edition of *The Oliver Wight Class A Standard for Business Excellence.*

47

CHAPTER CONTENT

Driven by Strategy

Shaped to Organizational Needs

Process Structure and Elements

Insights and Knowledge

Integration and Optimization

Technology Enabled

Behaviors and Competencies

Performance Measurement

DRIVEN BY STRATEGY

1. **Integrated Business Planning is the strategy deployment mechanism for the business. The process is designed to reference strategy continuously. Strategy drives the process, and the process informs strategy.**

   a. Strategy as the Driver

   Strategy provides the direction and framework against which proposed plans and actions are tested, and decisions are made. Strategic Business Objectives have been identified and are monitored throughout the process.

   b. Strategic Monitoring

   The status of strategic programs and assumptions is monitored to enable continuous review. Changes are identified early, and the impact on the business, including resources and financial performance, is evaluated.

   c. Gap-Closing Activity

   Gaps between the latest bottom-up view and strategic roadmaps are a specific focus for each process review, resulting in gap-closing activities.

   d. Strategy Closed Loop

   Changes to key business facts and insights that could impact the strategic direction are identified and addressed through the process.

2. **The process enables natural Strategic Management.**

   a. Strategy Is Lived

   Strategy pertinent to each process review is explicit. All participants understand and can articulate the strategy, the key underlying assumptions, and the impact on the business. The natural outcome is that strategy directs all plans and activities.

   b. Extended Empowerment

   The scope of empowerment includes the strategic context. Thinking and decision making naturally connect to strategic outcomes at all levels.

SHAPED TO ORGANIZATIONAL NEEDS

3. The process comprises a series of integrated and interdependent business reviews. IBP will continue to evolve to meet the changing structure and accountabilities of the business.

   a. The Process Reflects Organizational Accountabilities

      The process is structured in support of business accountabilities. The executive team member accountable for the relevant strategy roadmap owns and chairs his/ her respective element of the process.

   b. Whole of Business

      IBP ensures that all business activities and plans are synchronized in pursuit of the company's strategic plan. The process is structured to integrate all elements of the business, including enabling services such as Talent Management, Learning and Development, and Information Technology.

   c. Global, Regional, Multi-Entity, or Matrix Businesses

      In global, regional, multi-entity, or matrix organizations, process design has been appropriately applied to enable an effective monthly process in this more complex environment. It assures process flow across disparate organizational or matrix accountabilities and geographies and aligns with or clarifies decision rights. Such a process will conclude with a Corporate Business Review.

   d. Decision Rights

      Formal decision rights have been established for each process element within the matrix. This ensures decisions are made at the right level and drive empowerment.

   e. Phase 1 Capability

      Phase 1 capability has been achieved in all subprocesses.

4. The IBP process shape evolves in support of customer value and segmentation.

   a. Customer Value

      As businesses gain a clear understanding of customer value, there is likely to be an organizational response. Change in organization structure and emphasis is reflected in the IBP process design to ensure it continues to be fit for purpose as the business management process to deliver the strategy.

b. Segmentation

Customer/market segmentation or supply chain segmentation will often require organizational and accountability change. Such changes are reflected in the IBP process design.

c. Collaborative Partners

Where customer or supplier collaboration exists, the process structure enables the appropriate inclusion of these partners.

PROCESS STRUCTURE AND ELEMENTS

5. **The Product Management Review is owned and chaired by the executive accountable for the Product and Portfolio Roadmap. The review assesses current performance with product and portfolio plans by business segment to deliver commitments and deploy the Product and Portfolio Roadmap. The focus is on driving up the value of the product portfolio and better aligning with customer/consumer needs.**

a. Positioning

The Product Management Review is where plans to deploy the Product and Portfolio Roadmap are reviewed, change is understood, and actions to close gaps to commitments are agreed.

b. Strategic Focus

Focus is on deploying the Product and Portfolio Roadmap over the IBP horizon of typically 24 to 36 months, encompassing the next two fiscal year-ends. The Strategic Plan is the driver of all considerations.

c. Key Elements

The Product Management Review includes an understanding of product development funnel health, project prioritization and filtering, resource balancing, current and projected portfolio health, financial outcome, and strategic alignment.

6. **The Demand Review is owned and chaired by the executive accountable for the Market Roadmap. The review assesses current performance with customer and market plans by business segment to deliver commitments and deploy the Market Roadmap. The focus is on driving the revenue and margin for the business and identifying opportunities in support of growth consistent with strategy.**

   a. Positioning

      The Demand Review is where plans to drive revenue and margin are reviewed, change is understood, and actions to close gaps to commitments are agreed.

   b. Strategic Focus

      Focus is on deploying the Market Roadmap over the IBP horizon of typically 24 to 36 months, encompassing the next two fiscal year-ends. The Strategic Plan is the driver of all considerations.

   c. Key Elements

      The Demand Review includes an understanding of actions necessary to drive demand, development of assumptions and insights, modeling of scenarios, driving opportunity management, and management of vulnerabilities.

7. **The Supply Chain Review is owned and chaired by the executive accountable for supply commitments and strategy. The review assesses current performance with supply plans to deliver on commitments and deploy the Supply Chain Roadmap. The focus is on creating competitive advantage through a Lean and Agile Supply Chain optimized to deliver the requirements of product and demand plans.**

   a. Positioning

      The Supply Chain Review is where plans to deliver the requirements of the product and demand plans are reviewed, change is understood, and actions to close gaps to commitments are agreed. Segmented Supply Chain Capability Reviews exist to provide an understanding of demonstrated and projected capability, both owned and key third-party suppliers.

   b. Strategic Focus

      Focus is on deploying the Supply Chain Roadmap over the IBP horizon of typically 24 to 36 months, encompassing the next two fiscal year-ends. The Strategic Plan is the driver of all considerations.

c. Key Elements

The Segmented Supply Chain Capability Review includes an understanding of demonstrated performance and improvement plans. The Supply Chain Review includes an understanding of Supply Chain capability and improvements, inventory or lead-time strategies and planning assumptions, modeling of alternative supply plans, balancing to resources, and financial implications.

8. **Integration and Optimization is a continuous process deployed to address key issues and opportunities for the business and to reoptimize in response to change.**

a. Positioning

Integration and Optimization proactively identifies significant gaps and opportunities when comparing the latest bottom-up view to the Business Plan and strategy and manages gap-closing or opportunity-conversion solutions or recommendations for the business. In addition, it is the driver of formal Continuous Improvement in both process and content for the IBP process as a whole.

b. Strategic Focus

Focus is on reoptimizing the business in line with the Strategic Plan.

c. Key Elements

The Integration and Optimization process includes identification of significant changes in business projections versus Business Plan and strategy, assumptions, insights, vulnerabilities and opportunities, strategic initiatives, and business (governance) risks. There is active management of changes as they are identified through the process and proactive management of broader business issues over the full IBP horizon. Modeling of scenarios is a key feature in developing solutions to optimize the business as a whole in line with strategy.

d. The Integration and Optimization Review

The review is owned and chaired by the Integrated Business Planning Process Leader for the business entity. The review pulls together the full financial picture for the business, along with the relevant focus, key issues, solutions, and decisions to be made at the Management Business Review (MBR).

9. **The Management Business Review is owned and chaired by the business leader and comprises the Leadership Team. The review assesses current business performance and projections by business segment to deliver commitments and deploy strategy. There is intense focus on external dynamics and insights, resulting opportunities and business risks, and the modeling of scenarios to deliver optimized business performance.**

   a. Positioning

   The MBR is the crucial element of the monthly governance process where current and projected business performance is managed and optimized: Strategy is driven, change is understood, the outcomes from modeled opportunities and implications are reviewed, and decisions are made to optimize business performance, with business risks managed and mitigated.

   b. Strategic Focus

   Focus is on deploying the business strategy over the IBP horizon of typically 24 to 36 months, encompassing the next two fiscal year-ends. Strategy is the driver of all considerations.

   c. Corporate Business Review (Where Applicable)

   In a multi-entity, corporate/group environment with multiple Management Business Reviews, a Corporate Business Review is conducted to assess the optimized outcome for the corporation/group. This comprises the Chief Executive Officer and Corporate Executive Leadership Team. The focus is shareholder value over a longer-term horizon and corporate strategy deployment, including investment/trade-off decisions.

INSIGHTS AND KNOWLEDGE

10. **Capture of Insights and their implications is recognized as crucial to proactive, longer-term management of the business.**

    a. Strategic Drivers

    Through the Strategic Planning process, the business will identify its key business and market drivers, such as industry growth, strategic partnerships, competitor dynamics, market or geographical penetration, and product innovation, as well as political, environmental, or regulatory factors.

Assumptions and Insights will be determined for each driver. These are well communicated to ensure common understanding and consensus and underpin roadmaps and business projections, and there is ongoing management through the IBP process.

b. Management of External Drivers and Capture of Knowledge

Management of business and market Assumptions and Insights is a formal process with accountability assigned for each. Sources are identified to monitor trends, analysis, and commentary such that knowledge and facts are captured to enhance understanding and effectiveness, thereby, enabling learning and improvement.

c. Planning and Modeling

Assumptions and Insights and their implications are time phased through the planning horizon. They are modeled and provide the basis for evaluation of longer-term plans, thereby, establishing a clear relationship between the driver and the consequential business outcome.

d. Proactive Management

New knowledge will result in challenging whether current Assumptions/ Insights have changed. Changes in Assumptions/Insights and their implications, including potential business (governance) risk, are modeled through the process to identify impact and appropriate response. This ensures changes to key drivers are proactively managed well in advance of any execution activity.

INTEGRATION AND OPTIMIZATION

11. **Integration of Business Plans is driven by analysis and understanding of outputs from the core processes and inputs from the enabling functions, including Talent Management, Learning and Development, and Information Technology.**

a. Financial Integration

Decision making and business reporting are supported by financial projections through the IBP horizon. Financial assumptions are explicit. Financial opportunities and risks are proactively managed and mitigated. Focus is on direction versus precision.

b. Integration of Enabling Functions

The IBP cycle has been designed to incorporate inputs from all support functions/enabling processes. This ensures full transparency of their ability to support the IBP plan, to identify gaps and opportunities, and to establish full alignment to enable solutions and decisions.

c. Management of Aspirational Targets

Business aspirations supporting corporate objectives, including stretch goals and targets, are included in the IBP plans and form the basis for gap-closing activity and modeling. Improved opportunity conversion enables response to new or changed targets with minimal disruption.

d. Strategic Initiatives

The process has full transparency of strategic programs and projects. Issues and constraints are managed early and effectively to ensure the overall progression remains on track.

e. Prioritization

Prioritization decisions are driven by Strategic Business Objectives and are taken to optimize the whole business. The process provides options and recommendations with associated impact, including any necessary trade-offs, to realign Business Plans and investments.

12. **The focus of the Integration and Optimization process is on providing the business optimization choices based on modeling of scenarios and outcomes.**

a. Working with a Range of Outcomes

The Integration and Optimization process enables the organization to better manage uncertainty. Modeling of scenarios delivers a range of outcomes based on internal and external factors. Modeling capability enables plans that increasingly optimize the business.

b. Use of Analytics and Modeling

Critical insights in support of learning and decision making are gathered using data analytics. Analytics and modeling are routinely deployed throughout the IBP process to optimize the projected performance of the business. Necessary trade-offs are clearly articulated and their impact understood, ensuring optimized solutions are selected in line with strategy.

13. **The Integration and Optimization Team, led by the IBP Process Leader, works collaboratively across the organization to develop solutions and model alternative scenarios. Its objective is to optimize the business performance in line with Strategic Business Objectives.**

    a. Competencies

    The people on the team understand the business and strategic drivers. They bring facts and perspective. They are proactive in identifying and prioritizing gaps and opportunities and in developing solutions. The team has the capability to deploy analytics and modeling to understand potential business impacts and bring the solution that is right for the business.

    b. Team Members

    The core team drives the process and content of IBP. Team membership is determined in line with business evolution to ensure the best input and contribution.

TECHNOLOGY ENABLED

14. **Technology supporting the IBP process is integrated but separate from execution systems, acting as the single source of truth for integrated planning, modeling of scenarios, decision making, and reporting.**

    a. Integrated

    The technology supports simultaneous, team-based planning and allows for ease of connectivity to a variety of data sources, for example, ERP system, best-of-breed tools, project management systems, and financial systems, to supports changing business environments.

    b. Capability

    Although the ability to aggregate and disaggregate selectively from source systems exists, the technology is not beholden to detailed sources for aggregate planning and modeling of scenarios.

    c. Graphical

    The tool contains a user interface for modeling and allows for graphical output of plans, facilitating greater understanding and decision making.

d. Single Source of Information

Technology acts as a repository for approved IBP plans and the modeled ranges of outcomes. This means both the planning software tool as well as the data storage location are established to store IBP-related reports and information packs.

e. Security

The technology supports security and confidentiality of information.

15. **Technology is able to store, use, and make visible multiple inputs for modeling scenarios and supporting the resulting plans with pertinent information.**

a. Inputs

Insights, risks, vulnerabilities, and opportunities can be stored, managed, and measured in the database.

b. Use

The tool has the functionality to use multiple inputs and algorithms to drive scenario modeling, with linkages that allow for changes in inputs to drive changes in outputs.

c. Visibility

Inputs are clearly visible and documented within each resulting plan.

16. **The IBP technology is easy to use and allows for rapid planning and modeling of scenarios in response to internal and external dynamics and changes in insights.**

a. Rapid

Technology supports agile scenario modeling within the continuous Integration and Optimization process.

b. Ease of Use

Technology is designed for ease of use and configuration and is able to be operated by a variety of business users with sensitivity to frequent changes in organization and roles.

BEHAVIORS AND COMPETENCIES

17. IBP is a team-based process, supporting the Business Values, demonstrating effective group dynamics, breadth of organizational involvement, preparation and participation, open sharing, commitment, and accountability.

a. Leadership

Leadership for this management style is paramount and will determine its success. Leadership and commitment are demonstrated throughout the process by reinforcing direction and ambition, establishing end-to-end thinking, and creating an environment for structured Continuous Improvement and empowerment.

b. Collective Behavioral Responsibility

A team-based style drives a business rather than functional perspective. Collective decision making and problem solving are natural characteristics.

c. Accountability

Performance is measured, and accountability for delivery of commitments and deployment of strategy is clear.

d. Empowerment

The framework of the process empowers decision making. The process drives broad-based and increased involvement in business management and deployment of strategy with decision making at the appropriate level in the process, and issues are elevated by exception. Feedback to all involved in the process is routine.

18. The organization recognizes that there are particular competencies to manage and sustain the process at this level. Plans exist to ensure that these competencies are developed and retained.

a. Situational Leadership

The Leadership Team adapt their style given a range of opportunities and challenges while driving increasing empowerment within a growing organizational maturity.

b. Planning for Sustainability and Continuity

For the process to be sustainable, it is inherent that all new employees are educated to understand that IBP is "the way we run the business." Key stakeholders in the process are inducted to understand the IBP style of management. Succession planning ensures key participants in the process, such as facilitators, are naturally replaced as incumbents move on in their career.

c. Managing Ambiguity

Across all elements of the process, uncertainty is expected and is managed. Players in the process are developing increasing competence to support this world.

d. Modeling and Analysis

Modeling a range of outcomes becomes natural in an organization striving to optimize its performance. Modeling and analytical capabilities exist, at least within a core group in the process, especially within those engaged in Integration and Optimization.

e. Business Finance

At this level of maturity, where the Annual Plan/Budget is derived directly from IBP, *Beyond Budgeting* directs Financial Management increasingly toward optimization activity and, hence, a broader-based business perspective.

PERFORMANCE MEASUREMENT

19. There is a hierarchy of balanced measures that monitors the effective deployment of the Strategic Plan and the performance of the business. There is clear ownership of and accountability for each Key Performance Indicator. These measures are used to focus attention on areas of the business that require action to achieve performance targets or to optimize the business.

a. Business Scorecard

A set of Key Performance Indicators has been identified that measure the critical elements for the delivery of strategy and business governance, for which the Leadership Team hold themselves accountable. This Business Scorecard is reviewed at the Management Business Review.

b. Review Scorecard

A suite of Key Performance Indicators has been identified for each business review within IBP. Each review scorecard will include some Key Performance Indicators taken from the Business Scorecard as well as a broader range of KPIs applicable to that element of the process.

c. Use of Key Performance Indicators

   Key Performance Indicators are used for learning and to identify performance improvement and business optimization opportunities.

20. Process measures have been defined within the balanced hierarchy. These monitor the performance of key processes that enable business performance. The specifics of these key process measures will vary based on industry, strategy, and Value Proposition. Targets have been set and improvements are being achieved.

a. Process Measures Defined

   Process measures and associated Key Performance Indicators have been defined and include, for example, portfolio balance and vitality, conversion of commercial opportunities, rolled throughput yield in the supply chain, agility, flexibility, and Talent Management.

b. Measured Process Results Are Acted Upon

   Teams own the analyzed gaps between desired and actual performance in core process areas. The measures demonstrate process improvement and are benchmarked to industry standards.

21. Business performance measures are defined in the balanced hierarchy. Targets have been set, and improvements are being achieved.

a. Business Performance Addresses Status and Achievement of Strategy

   Key business measures include sales revenue, profitability, cash, return on capital, and customer satisfaction.

b. Performance is Managed with a Continuous Improvement Mind-Set

   Performance toward established targets is monitored, gaps are identified, and corrective actions are taken. Routine achievement of established targets calls for renewal of those targets to enable increased performance to sustain or improve competitive advantage.

5

MANAGING THE PRODUCTS
AND SERVICES PORTFOLIO

PURPOSE

To support the Strategic Plan through the development and implementation of an optimized products and services. The portfolio with deliver customer value, optimal performance, and financial goals enabled through sustained Class A capability and performance.

POSITIONING

Product and Portfolio Management includes all aspects of planning and managing the company's Products and Services Portfolio: customer and consumer insights, market roadmaps, product and portfolio roadmaps, product and portfolio planning, ideation, management of the innovation funnel, program and project management, resource management, product development and launch, portfolio management, and product life-cycle management.

Process maturity improves over time through education, committed leadership, expert guidance, and a focused effort to attain key business milestones.

After embarking on the path to improvement, accountabilities are assigned, the elements and characteristics of the processes are implemented, and targeted measures drive improvement to enable process transformation.

Done well, a Class A Milestone is achieved at the top of Phase 1 of Business Maturity (see Foundation, Figure I.1). At this stage, the Product and Portfolio Roadmaps drive product portfolio and life-cycle planning to ensure product succession. Product plans are fully integrated and effective to increase launch success. Programs and projects are

63

managed through team-based Project Management, including the early involvement of customers and suppliers.

From this Class A Milestone vantage point, we introduce the next level of maturity in the seventh edition of *The Oliver Wight Class A Standard for Business Excellence.*

Within this chapter, the term *product* is used to refer to both products and services.

CHAPTER CONTENT

Driven by Strategy

Integration

Product and Portfolio Management and Marketing

Managing and Optimizing the Portfolio

Managing Programs and Projects

Team-Based Project Management and Concurrency

Program and Project Resource Planning

Managing Technology and Innovation

Behavior and Competencies

Performance Measurement

DRIVEN BY STRATEGY

1. **The Strategic Plan includes marketing, product and portfolio, supply, and finance strategies and is used to develop a Product and Portfolio Roadmap, which includes a Technology Roadmap. The combined direction drives Product and Portfolio Planning and execution.**

   a. Congruence with Strategic Plan

      The leader accountable for managing the Products and Services Portfolio uses the Strategic Plan to develop a Product and Portfolio Roadmap that drives Portfolio Management and optimization.

   b. Value Proposition and Value Disciplines

      The Product and Portfolio Roadmap fully aligns with the Value Proposition and Value Discipline focus.

   c. Congruence with Market Roadmap

      All product and service development is directed by the Market Roadmap and translated by the Product and Portfolio Roadmap into actions.

   d. Competitive Analysis

      The Product and Portfolio Roadmap is updated at least annually with the new insights derived from an analysis of the competition and industry standards.

   e. Technology Roadmap

      The Technology Roadmap identifies the core technologies and capabilities to fulfill the company strategy and defines the company's research and development and investment programs.

2. **The Product and Portfolio Roadmap guides products, brands, platforms, product life cycles, and technology deployment.**

   a. Brand Deployment

      The Product and Portfolio Roadmap deploys the brand strategy through a clearly defined, multi-year timeline.

b. Product Platforms

Products with similar characteristics and requirements are grouped into platforms, and the plan for each is clear and consistent with the aggregate plan.

c. Life-Cycle Management

A process exists to monitor and predict life-cycle trends and, therefore, support planned product introduction and phase-out.

d. Technology Deployment

Opportunities for new and available technologies are identified in support of the Product and Portfolio Roadmap, and plans exist to drive maximum return from technology investment across the business.

INTEGRATION

3. **Product plans are assessed, balanced to capability, and managed through a monthly Product Review process. Integration with Demand Management, Supply Management, and Financial Planning is ensured through an Integrated Business Planning process.**

a. Process Mechanism

The linkage between Product and Portfolio Management and the other elements in the integrated planning process is defined and made explicit.

b. Linkages

The Product and Portfolio Management process ensures the volume and value projections related to changes to the portfolio are updated at least monthly based on the latest project plans and their business cases. The updated numbers, and supporting assumptions, are provided to Demand, Supply, and Finance and used by each of them as inputs to their plans and projections.

c. Gap Management and Assumptions

An Assumptions Database is maintained to enable gaps to be analyzed and understood based on the thinking used to establish current plans. Assumptions are used to ensure plans are adjusted only if new information is better than that used initially.

d. Linkage to Reconciliation Management

Product and Portfolio Management develops business solutions when its proposed plans identify business gaps or risks that are deemed unacceptable.

4. **Processes exist to forge the operating links between day-to-day planning and execution, providing visibility and control of uncertainty and enabling consistent and improving performance in support of business goals.**

a. Product and Portfolio Management Defined

Product and Portfolio Management process maps have been converted to Value Stream Maps to ensure the purpose and the value of each step are understood and, hence, a true Lean capability can be exploited.

b. Fully Integrated with Core Processes

Processes share real-time information to enable decisions to be made at the optimal time.

c. Performance Gap Management

Timely adjustments to Assumptions enable performance gaps to be identified for decisions and action.

d. Modeling and Analytics

Modeling and analytics methodologies are developed and deployed to enable ongoing optimization of the portfolio.

PRODUCT AND PORTFOLIO MANAGEMENT AND MARKETING

5. **Information is provided about all targeted markets to help create or modify roadmaps. These roadmaps are aligned with business goals.**

a. Markets, Sectors, Segments, and Channels

There is a process to understand the characteristics of the chosen markets, sectors, segments, and channels to keep product development aligned with market requirements.

b. Portfolio Plan

   The Portfolio Plan is time phased and defines the portfolio of current products, additions to the portfolio through product launches, and removals from the portfolio through product phase-outs.

c. Funnel Health

   The number and type of projects at each development stage are balanced and aligned to the Product and Portfolio Roadmap for sustaining the business and meeting growth and margin objectives.

d. Market Position

   Market position and profitability are understood by markets, sectors, segments, and channels for the current portfolio. Gaps are identified through updates in Assumptions, and actions are taken to ensure planned business goals are achieved.

e. Segmentation

   A segmentation approach has been implemented to optimize customer and consumer service. The portfolio has been structured to support this approach consistent with the Strategic Plan and Roadmaps.

6. **Techniques are used to create understanding of both customer and consumer future needs to develop a Value Chain response.**

a. Gaining Insights into Customer and Consumer Needs

   An Insights process gains knowledge of customer and consumer needs as expressed, deduced, or created to keep the product portfolio competitive.

b. Anticipating Customer and Consumer Needs

   Insights enable Product and Portfolio Management to anticipate customer and consumer needs, including unanticipated needs.

c. Creating the Value Chain

   Customer-understood value is embedded in the Supply Chain, enabling a Value Chain to be established.

MANAGING AND OPTIMIZING THE PORTFOLIO

7. There is an understanding of product life cycles that drives the portfolio to support the Product and Portfolio Roadmap.

a. Portfolio Management

A process exists to maintain alignment of the portfolio to the Market Roadmap and supply capability.

b. Balancing the Projects

The mix of products that are existing, new, and under development is reviewed to ensure the right balance of projects to maintain a competitive portfolio aligned to business goals. Considerations include innovation, risk, and timing.

c. Proactive Product Phase-Out

Life-cycle maps identify when product phase-out should be initiated. Product phase-out is actively managed.

8. There is a Business Filtering process to ensure the most effective use of resources. The process ensures selection, prioritization, and resourcing of active projects.

a. Projects Prioritization

A defined Prioritization process exists for the ranking of all active projects and projects waiting for authorization.

b. Prioritization Process Considerations

The Prioritization process criteria include a number of business drivers, such as strategy, return on investment, feasibility, risk, and profitability and are not based solely on financial measures.

c. Business Filter

A Business Filtering process uses the prioritization mechanism to ensure optimal use of resources for authorized and pending projects.

d. Filter Criteria

Pass/fail rates are monitored along the funnel to regularly challenge and update filter criteria and the Prioritization process.

MANAGING PROGRAMS AND PROJECTS

9. Formal processes exist to manage programs and projects to achieve the Product and Portfolio Roadmap. These may be centralized through a Program Management Office.

a. Program and Project Management

All Programs and Projects are planned and managed through a formal process to ensure the best use of resources and competencies and to achieve business goals.

b. Decision Checkpoints

The program and project control process includes formal decision checkpoints to determine the progression of Programs and Projects to the next stage.

c. Cost Control Process

A formal cost control process is used to ensure that Programs and Projects are developed and launched within their approved budget.

d. Managing the Launch

The decision to launch is supported by a formal prelaunch checklist that is used to minimize launch execution risk.

e. Tactical Launch

Launch plans and timing are defined based on the latest insights gained from the market, customers, and competition.

f. Post-Launch Review

Formal post-launch reviews are conducted following market reaction, when learnings and benefits can be maximized, to ensure future programs and projects take advantage of these experiences for future development and introductions.

g. Attrition

The number of ideas that begin as projects, but fail to pass decision checkpoints, is monitored to establish the attrition rate of the funnel. This rate is used to ensure that there is sufficient flow of ideas to ensure there are no funnel gaps.

h. Program and Project Handovers

Program and project handovers have been clearly defined to ensure the effective transfer of accountability.

i. Business Improvement

The Product and Portfolio Roadmap is supported by a company-wide commitment to continuously improve the product development and delivery process.

10. Program Management is applied to the integration and synchronization of multiple interdependent projects.

a. Program Management Process

The concept of Program Management is well understood and applied to situations that require the integration of multiple interdependent projects.

b. Alignment with the Product and Portfolio Roadmap

There is an agreed plan among the program partners (internal and external) regarding achievement of the program goals that are aligned to the Product and Portfolio Roadmap.

c. Program Synchronization

Program Management deploys appropriate tools to synchronize all projects that are integrated into the program.

d. Service Level Agreements

Formal Service Level Agreements are used to define deliverables for the program, and Key Performance Indicators validate they are being followed.

11. All authorized and pending projects are formally managed through the Master Product Development Plan to meet the business goals.

a. Unconstrained View

An unconstrained view for programs and projects is used to ensure the Master Product Development Plan (MPDP). When this plan does not satisfy the Strategic Plan, gap-closing opportunities are identified and modeled.

b. Master Product Development Plan

   The MPDP communicates the order and priority of approved projects and includes anticipated future activity to resolve resource conflicts.

c. Master Product Development Plan Scope

   The MPDP provides all the information required to effectively integrate with Demand, Supply, and Finance to support their planning and decision making.

d. Horizon

   At a minimum, the MPDP provides visibility of activities within the current Integrated Business Planning horizon.

12. **Program and Project Management processes use vulnerabilities and opportunities to enable modeling, escalation, and decision-making processes.**

a. Vulnerability and Opportunity

   The Program and Project vulnerability and opportunity database is used to determine parameters to support scenario planning for modeling and decision making.

b. Decision Escalation

   Decision making has been empowered throughout the organization, and there is a formal decision escalation process to obtain the required authority.

TEAM-BASED PROJECT MANAGEMENT AND CONCURRENCY

13. **The company has a team-based culture facilitating concurrent project design and development. This improves velocity and the ability to deliver and increases right-first-time performance.**

a. Team-Based Project Management

   Team-Based Project Management is used to facilitate sharing of knowledge and activities, enabling execution of work elements in parallel to accelerate time-to-market. Self-managed team capabilities are developing.

b. Extended Project Teams

   Project teams are extended as necessary and may include customers, consumers, suppliers, external technology owners, and regulatory experts.

c. Concurrency

   A concurrent approach is used to optimize time-to-market. This is demonstrated through team-based execution of activities in parallel.

d. Design for Supply

   Supply activities are introduced concurrently and as early as possible so that products are developed considering ease of supply.

e. Collaboration

   The environment enables natural sharing of information and data across all areas of the business and extended project teams. This ensures decision making is optimized to sustain Class A performance.

f. Drive the Future Organization

   The organization design has removed traditional functional and departmental barriers to support a team- or process-based structure.

PROGRAM AND PROJECT RESOURCE PLANNING

14. Aggregate resources are planned and optimized to achieve the Product and Portfolio Roadmap and support business goals.

a. Aggregate Resource Plan

   The Aggregate Resource Plan captures all critical resource needs. It uses established templates based on historical profiling. The plan is built on assumptions informed by past performance to model the future mix requirements.

b. Horizon

   At a minimum, the plan covers the horizon of the MPDP and must reflect the lead times to secure additional critical resources. Resource planning decisions are routinely made well in advance of requirements.

c. Resource Deployment

Multi-functional resources are managed to satisfy the requirements of the plan.

d. Resource Optimization

Where there is a conflict between multi-functional resource allocations, issues that cannot be resolved are modeled to enable decisions for optimal allocation.

e. Business Agility

Sufficient flexibility is available in the plan to support business opportunities that were not anticipated in roadmaps.

f. Resource Acquisition

Changes in headcount and critical skills are identified in the plan, and decisions are made to acquire the required resource mix.

MANAGING TECHNOLOGY AND INNOVATION

15. **The company understands and manages current and future technologies required to deliver the Product and Portfolio Roadmap.**

a. Current Technologies

The company understands and is investing in its technologies that underpin the business.

b. Future Technologies

The concept of the critical mass is established. Where new technology is important to the business but the required capability is not in place, decisions are made to secure the capability.

c. Supply Chain and Technology

The Supply Chain is a potential source of technology and competency. Partnerships are sought to enhance skill and competency to satisfy business requirements, and they are used to drive the technology development process.

16. Ideation, Innovation, and Knowledge Management provide a competitive advantage.

a. Ideation

   Sources of ideation extend beyond the boundaries of the organization, drawing from customers, consumers, suppliers, competition, and the marketplace in general. Ideation is a formal and thought-lead process.

b. Innovation

   Active programs are in place to convert prioritized ideas into applications that secure a competitive advantage.

c. Knowledge Management

   A culture exists to motivate the free flow of ideas and innovations through the organization as individual and team knowledge are accepted as ways to drive competitive advantage. This is enabled through a formal set of Knowledge Management practices.

BEHAVIOR AND COMPETENCIES

17. The required behaviors to optimize interactions have been established from the Business Values that enable a team-based culture and natural communication.

a. Rewards and Recognition

   A team-based culture has been established, enabling both individual and team activities to be recognized and rewarded to communicate successes.

b. Ownership and Accountability

   Employees have a clear understanding and ownership of the Strategic Plan, which enables them to establish teams when deviations from the plan are detected. The use of self-managed teams is encouraged by leadership, who hold the teams accountable through the allocation of required resources.

c. Communication

   The communication of information and data is technology enabled and has significantly reduced the need for meetings. Employees and teams naturally share their progress to accelerate learning.

d. Decisiveness

The environment enables sharing of information and data, in real time, which are then used by employees and teams to take action.

18. An environment exists that encourages individuals and expert teams to accept empowerment and take initiative.

a. Leadership for Business Excellence

Leaders foster an environment that systematically provides the required resources and skills to support the Product and Portfolio Roadmap. Empowered individuals and teams are a natural consequence, providing the knowledge and expertise to achieve business goals.

b. Situational Leadership

Predominant management style has evolved to Leadership increasing the use of delegation and empowerment and enabling different styles of management/leadership to be used. This has eliminated traditional organizational barriers, enabling the successful use of multi-functional teams and concurrency.

c. Knowledge-Based Processes

Knowledge captured in the processes makes them intuitive and self-sustaining.

d. Teams

Team and Process-Based thinking has become a natural way of life; self-directed teams are developing. Teams hold themselves accountable to deliver results on time. This capability enables programs and projects to be successfully managed and delivered.

e. Culture

The inclusive environment and empowerment at all levels ensure shared knowledge, understanding, and application. Decisions are moving more to a consensus basis. Trust has been earned up and down the organization.

19. **Competencies are unique skills, talents, and proficiencies to ensure individual, team, and organizational success. Competencies are developed to support current and future needs, in both development and delivery.**

    a. Developing Talent, Skills, and Competencies

    The talent, skills, and competencies required to undertake current and future needs of Product and Portfolio Management are understood. This includes competency in optimization of Program Management, Project Management, and Regulatory compliance.

    b. Collaboration with the Supply Chain

    Collaboration has become the basis to ensure new knowledge is embedded in process designs and that learnings are shared.

    c. New Technology Implementation

    Development plans are in place for the talent, skills, and competencies required for new technology to be implemented.

    d. Portfolio Management

    Product Portfolios are managed through internal knowledge of product capabilities, applications, and performance as well as external evaluation of information from the market, competition, and customers.

20. **The organization has evolved to enable behaviors, teamwork, and decision rights that best support delivery of the Product and Portfolio Roadmap.**

    a. Customer Focus

    There is a passion for customers' success based on an understanding of their requirements. The organizational structure enables collaboration.

    b. Structure

    The organization has evolved into a broader, flatter structure, which provides a responsive and agile capability with greatly simplified communication through fewer layers.

    c. Promotions and Rewards

    The organization values and recognizes gaining skills and taking initiative to increase responsibilities.

d. Roles and Responsibilities

Roles and responsibilities and associated decision rights are regularly redefined to align their scope in response to organization changes.

e. Management of a Virtual Organization

The organization has developed a capability to manage a virtual organization to better respond to new challenges and collaboration.

PERFORMANCE MEASUREMENT

21. **A balanced hierarchy of measures that has targets and time-phased improvement has been defined by Product and Portfolio Management. These measures are critical to Business Excellence, to drive competitive advantage, to the delivery of the Product and Portfolio Roadmap, and to creation of the Business Scorecard.**

a. Measures Defined and Understood

A balanced suite of measures has been defined, and targets are based on external benchmarking where possible and support achievement of the Product and Portfolio Roadmap. The measures have been communicated to all stakeholders.

b. Reviewed

The key measures are reviewed to align improvement projects to the Product and Portfolio Roadmap and achievement of Critical Success Factors. Key Performance Indicators and targets are changed to maintain visibility and prioritize improvement.

c. Hierarchical Linkage

There is a clear hierarchical link between the suite of key measures for each business process and the Business Scorecard. Once process proficiency has been established, the measures are delegated or redefined, or the targets revised.

d. Competitive Advantage

Key measures and associated Key Performance Indicators are a competitive advantage rather than a goal and drive individual and team-based behaviors.

e. Balance

A reasonable balance of measures exists among process areas. Leading indicators are increasingly used.

f. Evolving

It is recognized that when percentile performance is insufficient to determine improvements, a migration to Six Sigma methodology/statistical performance is required.

22. Process measures are valued and used by the Product and Portfolio Organization to drive and demonstrate delivery of the Roadmaps. Process measures are agreed in advance to ensure Class A performance.

a. Suite of Process Measures

There is a suite of measures for ideation, program and project effectiveness, Resource Management, and product development covering the full scope of Product and Portfolio Management.

b. Perfect Project Delivery

Perfect Project Delivery is viewed as a vital measure for Product and Portfolio Management performance. Percentage of projects delivered completely to cost, specification, launch date, and initial volumes, as compared to the business case at the go-to-development gate, is measured and is improving.

c. People Measures/Team-Based Measures

Measures in place recognize the importance of key skills to be developed in support of the Strategic Plan. These measures should capture, for example, the positioning of skill sets versus plan, percentage utilization of critical resources, retention of critical resources, and percentage of the project resourced appropriately for success.

23. Business performance measures are established in recognition that process measurement alone is insufficient. Business performance measures are agreed to ensure Class A performance and ensure value to stakeholders.

a. Strategic Alignment

Strategic Plan alignment is confirmed through the Critical Success Factors Roadmap.

b. Financial

    Financial success is confirmed through plan attainment and is monitored through Integrated Business Planning.

c. Variance to Plan

    Variance to plan is understood in both financial and operational performance terms.

d. Product Performance Management

    Performance of product and services in the marketplace and with customers is routinely measured and managed.

e. Responsiveness

    The importance of Velocity to deliver a real competitive advantage is understood. There is a focus on improving responsiveness to market competitive expectations, demonstrated by an improving trend in time-to-market, time-to-volume, and time-to-profit.

6

MANAGING MARKET DEMAND

PURPOSE

To deploy the Value Proposition to the marketplace to achieve Strategic Business Objectives. To ensure the market needs are understood with effective response from the organization and its partners. To deliver financial goals enabled though sustained Class A capability and performance.

POSITIONING

Market Demand Management encompasses how the business meets the needs, wants, and expectations of customers wherever they reside in the Value Chain.

Process maturity improves over time through education, committed leadership, expert guidance, and a focused effort to attain key business milestones.

Many companies begin their Class A improvement journey in a disconnected state, marked by functional silos, defensive behaviors, a disproportionate focus on the past, and a lack of clarity about the future. After embarking on the path to improvement, accountabilities are assigned, the elements and characteristics of the processes are implemented, and targeted measures drive improvement to enable process transformation.

Done well, a Class A Milestone is achieved at the top of Phase 1 of Business Maturity (see Foundation, Figure I.1). At this stage, formal Market Segmentation is defined, the consensus Demand Plan is based on multiple views, bias has been eliminated, and Demand Plan accuracy is improving. Volume, value, and margin are integrated and aligned, underpinned by assumptions, analytics, knowledge of vulnerability, and opportunity management supported by scenario planning.

From this Class A Milestone vantage point, it is possible to introduce this next level of maturity in the seventh edition of *The Oliver Wight Class A Standard for Business Excellence.*

CHAPTER CONTENT

Driven by Strategy

Integration

Modeling and Analytics

Market Segment Planning

Customer Collaboration

Market Segment Plan Execution

Demand Review Preparation

Demand Execution

Technology

Behavior and Competencies

Performance Measurement

DRIVEN BY STRATEGY

1. **The Strategic Plan includes Market, Product and Portfolio, Supply Chain, and Finance Strategies. These have been used to develop a Market Roadmap, which includes a Market Segment Roadmap. The combined direction is used to plan and drive market, channel, and customer activities.**

   a. Congruence with Strategic Plan

   The accountable leader for managing market demand uses the Strategic Plan to develop a Market Roadmap that drives market management.

   b. Value Proposition and Value Disciplines

   The Market Roadmap and supporting Market Segment Roadmaps fully align with the Value Proposition and Value Discipline focus.

   c. Competitive Analysis

   The Market Roadmap is updated at least annually with insights derived from an analysis of the competition and industry standards.

2. **Market Segment Roadmaps have been developed that further refine the Market Roadmap. These define how the business will address the market and how that will develop over the strategic horizon to deliver Strategic Business Objectives.**

   a. Understanding of Market Segments

   The business has a process for segmenting consumers and customers into homogenous groups who share similar needs, wants, and behaviors.

   b. Market Segment Roadmaps

   Market Segment Roadmaps have been developed that define how the business will address each Market Segment and how that will evolve over the strategic horizon to deliver Strategic Business Objectives. Key elements include portfolio offering, competencies, promotional support, product placement, and customer collaboration.

   c. Focus on Critical Success Factors

   Critical Success Factors have been identified for each Market Segment Roadmap. These are defined annually and drive planning, decisions, and actions within Marketing and Sales.

d. Ownership—Market Segment Roadmaps

   Market Segment Roadmaps are owned and deployed by Marketing and Sales.

e. Ownership—Detailed Marketing Mix Plans

   All activities surrounding portfolio offering, pricing, promotional activity, product placement, and required marketing and sales resources are owned by Marketing and Sales. These are reflected in the demand plan and monitored and managed through Integrated Business Planning (IBP).

INTEGRATION

3. Demand Plans are created, assessed, and managed through an ongoing Market Segment planning process, owned by Marketing and Sales. Integration with Product Management, Supply Management, and Financial Planning is ensured through Integrated Business Planning.

a. Process Mechanism

   The linkage between Demand Management and the other elements in IBP is defined and made explicit.

b. Linkages

   The Demand Management process ensures the volume, revenue, and margin projections are updated at least monthly. The updated numbers, with supporting Assumptions, are provided to the business and are used as inputs to the plans and projections.

c. Marketing Mix Investments

   Knowledge of the impact of marketing mix investments and effectiveness is developing and is used to improve analytical models. Demand Management proactively evaluates and adjusts investments in response to performance and market changes.

d. Linkage to Integration and Optimization

   Demand Management develops business solutions where the proposed plans identify business gaps or business risks that are deemed unacceptable.

e. Linkage to People Operations

   People Operations is a business partner to the Demand Management process and ensures that behaviors and competencies required to achieve the Market Segment Plans and the Demand Plans are being planned and developed.

f. Linkage to Business Improvement

Progress toward Business Improvement activities associated with Demand Management is reviewed at the monthly Demand Review.

4. Processes exist to forge the operating links between day-to-day planning and execution, providing visibility and control of uncertainty, and enabling consistence and improving performance in support of business goals.

a. Ongoing Monitoring

Actual demand is monitored, and change is responded to.

b. Fully Integrated with Core Processes

Processes share real-time information to enable decisions to be made at the optimal time.

c. Performance Gap Management

Timely adjustments to Assumptions enable performance gaps to be identified for decision and action.

MODELING AND ANALYTICS

5. The Marketing and Sales Teams are analyzing market data to generate insights to describe, predict, and improve sales and marketing performance. Analytics and predictive modeling are being used to drive greater understanding, create scenarios, and enable decision making.

a. Role of Analytics

Correlations between demand-driving parameters have been proven, enabling a good understanding of their cause and effect on marketing mix effectiveness and business results. Analytics are being used to develop predictive models, provide management information, and enable decisions through IBP.

b. Predictive Modeling

Predictive modeling is used by the Sales and Marketing Teams, providing multiple scenarios and options enabling appropriate adjustments to the Marketing Mix to support the achievement of Strategic Business Objectives. Predictive models are validated, and trust in the models is developing in the business teams.

c. Role of Demand Analyst

The Demand Analyst is a senior member of Sales and Marketing and is an expert in statistics, trend analysis, life-cycle planning, what-if analysis, and predictive modeling. The Analyst provides the Commercial Team with ongoing visibility and insight into macroeconomic and microeconomic trends, consumer and customer insights, and competitive intelligence.

MARKET SEGMENT PLANNING

6. **Rolling integrated Market Segment Plans, which cover categories, channels, customers, and consumers, are actively managed to deliver the Value Proposition and achieve the business goals over the Integrated Business Planning horizon.**

a. Value Chain

Market Segment Plans address the total offering across the Value Chain. Push/ pull activities are integrated, understood, and managed.

b. Characteristics

The Market Segment Plan demonstrates a complete integration of Sales and Marketing activities across the Value Chain. The plans clearly articulate positioning, portfolio offering, pricing, placement, promotion, people, physical evidence, and process.

c. Horizon and Granularity

The horizon and level of detail of the Market Segment Plans are consistent with IBP. The plans are expressed in volume, value, and margin.

d. Organization

Segment teams are established to focus on the Value Chain and deliver the business goals. Segment Teams typically include Demand Analysis, Insights, Channel and Customer Marketing, Brand, Sales, Finance, People Operations, Supply, and strategic partners.

e. Opportunity and Vulnerability Management

Opportunity and Vulnerability Management is an established and formal process used to proactively manage gaps and maximize business performance.

f. Monitoring

Business performance and customer/consumer experience are continuously monitored to ensure delivery of the Value Proposition. Key learnings and Insights are used to refine the plans.

CUSTOMER COLLABORATION

7. **Collaborative partnerships exist with strategic customers. Inter-Business Teams develop and execute Market Segment Plans.**

   a. Scope

   Strategic partnerships exist throughout the Value Chain. Collaboration ensures that customers and customers' needs are understood and embraced.

   b. Characteristics

   Clearly defined and agreed collaborative partnerships deliver shared objectives and benefits through joint Strategic Planning, Business Planning, and execution. Business Plans cover, at a minimum, the full IBP horizon. Real-time data are used across partnerships for planning, execution, and Performance Management.

   c. Organization

   Teams are established, which include business partners and functions, with documented shared goals, roles, responsibilities, and measures. Team members are organized to focus on daily, weekly, and monthly planning processes.

   d. Monitoring

   Business performance, along with customer and consumer experience, is continuously monitored to ensure delivery of the shared Value Proposition. Key learnings and Insights are used to refine Market Segment and Company Plans.

MARKET SEGMENT PLAN EXECUTION

8. **Detailed and time-phased Sales and Marketing activities exist to deliver the approved Market Segment Plan. These plans are integrated with the day-to-day and month-to-month activities of Sales and Marketing, including marketing activity management, account management, call cycles, and follow-up.**

   a. Time Phase

   Time phase is determined by the respective lead times to deploy specific Sales and Marketing Plans.

b. Detailed Activity Planning

The set of activities required to fulfill the Market Segment Plan is organized in a time-phased activity plan, allowing individuals to understand what they are responsible for, when it needs to be completed, and the interdependencies across activities.

c. Organization

There is a clear link and formal information flow between Segment Teams and Sales and Marketing Execution Teams.

d. Monitoring

Real-Time Insights gained from activity performance inform the Market Segment Team and lead to changes of both the Market Segment Plan and marketing activity levels.

DEMAND REVIEW PREPARATION

9. The Market Segment planning process culminates in a monthly Demand Review, a key element of Integrated Business Planning.

a. Demand Manager

The Demand Manager drives the monthly Preparation Cycle and Demand Review, identifying the key business issues, options, and outcomes. The Demand Manager works closely with the Market Segment Teams, Demand Analyst(s), Demand Execution Manager, Product Planning Manager, Supply Planning Manager, and the IBP Process Leader to ensure alignment of performance and plans to strategy.

b. Preparation

The Preparation Cycle incorporates key information and activities across all market segments: performance of market segment strategy and plans, changes in insights, modeling scenarios, adjusted segment plans, opportunities and vulnerabilities, consolidated financial projections, and gap-closing recommendations.

DEMAND EXECUTION

10. **Daily and weekly processes ensure that actual demand is proactively managed in line with Market Segment Plans and that the business can respond.**

    a. <u>Demand Execution Manager</u>

    The role includes management of specific issues in the near-term Demand Planning horizon when demand is greater than or less than planned. This involves identifying and resolving Abnormal Demand, managing Available to Promise, and monitoring Forecast Consumption. At a minimum, it enables a weekly review process.

    b. <u>Demand Sensing</u>

    Capabilities are established in the business using near real-time market information to respond effectively to changing demand signals and improve customer service levels.

    c. <u>Time Fences</u>

    Time fences are challenged to ensure decision points are driven closer to the point of delivery to enable a cost-effective, agile response.

    d. <u>Abnormal Demand</u>

    All orders are automatically evaluated against the Abnormal Demand rules embedded in the order entry system. Unexpected orders outside of defined tolerances are flagged for resolution by the Demand Execution Manager.

    e. <u>Order Management</u>

    Customer orders are routinely received, committed to, and fulfilled without human intervention. Order commitment is made systematically through Available-to-Promise/Capable-to-Promise functionality. Customer requests that cannot be satisfied are flagged with system-proposed alternatives.

    f. <u>Customer Segmentation</u>

    Customer segmentation defines service levels and is understood and managed across Segment Teams.

    g. <u>Customer Response</u>

    Speed to respond to and satisfy customer requests is improving through higher velocity that comes from system-based rules and segment prioritization.

h. Exception Reviews

Exception reviews occur as required to resolve issues and respond to unforeseen events that put customer service at risk.

TECHNOLOGY

11. Technology enables real-time access to data and Insights that provide the ability to make informed and timely business decisions.

a. Activity Management, Modeling, and Statistics

An actively used data repository has been enabled to capture demand history and the correlation between volumes, financials, market conditions, and activities to enable predictive modeling to be utilized based on changing market parameters. Variability is measured and understood.

b. Customer Relationship Management

A Customer Relationship Management tool is used to record customer intelligence and opportunities. The system provides the organization the ability to customize its marketing and selling activities to individual customer needs. The system is where all sales opportunities are made visible and prioritized.

c. Demand Planning and Execution

The Demand Planning system is integrated with business systems to enable Class A supply performance, valid order promising, and automated identification of Abnormal Demand.

d. Demand-Sensing Capability

Demand-sensing models utilizing the business's data repository and extrinsic information are used to remodel the near-term Demand Plan to support a rapid supply response.

BEHAVIOR AND COMPETENCIES

12. The behaviors that define the company's interactions have been established from Business Values that enable a team-based culture and natural communication.

a. Rewards and Recognition

A team-based culture has been established, enabling both individual and team activities to be recognized and rewarded to communicate successes.

b. Ownership and Accountability

Employees have a clear understanding and ownership of the Strategic Plan, which enables them to establish teams when deviations from the plan are detected. The use of self-managed teams is encouraged by leadership, who hold the teams accountable through the allocation of required resources.

c. Communication

The communication of information and data is technology enabled and has significantly reduced the need for meetings. Employees and teams naturally share their progress to accelerate learning.

d. Decisiveness

The environment enables sharing of information and data, in real-time, which is then used by employees and teams to act on.

13. **Competencies, talent, and skills are developed to support current and future needs. The organization drives the formation and empowerment of Market Segment Teams in pursuit of delivering the Value Proposition.**

a. Leadership

Leadership has the ability to interpret, blend, and construct plans based on knowledge of futuristic thinking, customer needs, and market segments, and are supported by Sales and Marketing competencies.

b. Segment Teams

Teams, which include partners outside the organization, are naturally formed and re-formed to suit changing business needs. Team behaviors support the natural flow of planning and activity while the organizational structure develops talent and capability to meet future business needs.

c. Developing Competencies, Talent, and Skills

The competencies, talent, and skills required to support current and future business needs are available. Plans and actions are in place to evolve or acquire new.

d. Positioning for Success and Adaptability

Predictive modeling and opportunities are used to articulate the range of potential business outcomes and develop a range of activities in response. There is confidence in committing to business results while recognizing that there is a range of potential outcomes. The organization exhibits flexibility and adaptability with continuous focus on business commitment by adjusting activities in response to market realities.

e. Knowledge-Based Processes

There is a desire to continuously increase knowledge of the market to apply and learn from insight in pursuit of business goals. Knowledge captured in the systems enables improved business decision making. Use of the knowledge systems is widespread.

f. Analytics and Modeling

The ability exists to develop analytical models to create predictive demand scenarios.

g. Planning and Execution

The ability exists to create time-phased Sales and Marketing activities that deliver Market Segment and Channel Plans. Execution competency should include marketing, sales, relationship management, and collaboration.

h. Improvement Mind-Set

The business strives for increased velocity in core business processes and customer response lead times.

PERFORMANCE MEASUREMENT

14. **A balanced hierarchy of key measures that have targets and time-phased improvement has been defined by the Demand Management organization. These measures are critical to Business Excellence that drives competitive advantage, the delivery of the Market Roadmap, and the creation of the Business Scorecard.**

a. Measures Defined and Understood

A balanced suite of measures has been defined. Targets are based on external benchmarking where possible and support achievement of the Market Roadmap. The measures have been communicated to all stakeholders and Market Segment Teams.

b. Reviewed

The key measures are regularly reviewed to align Demand Management activities to the Market Roadmap and achievement of Critical Success Factors.

Key Performance Indicators and targets are changed to maintain visibility and prioritize improvement.

c. Hierarchical Linkage

There is a clear hierarchical link between the suite of key measures for each business process and the Business Scorecard. Once process proficiency has been established, the measures are delegated or redefined, or the targets are revised.

d. Competitive Advantage

Key measures and associated Key Performance Indicators are a competitive advantage rather than a goal, and drive individual and team-based behaviors.

e. Balance

A reasonable balance of measures exists among process areas.

15. **Process measures are valued and used by the Demand Management organization to identify and provide focus to Demand Management process improvement. Process measures are agreed in advance to ensure Class A performance.**

a. Demand Planning Capability Performance

There is a suite of measures to measure the effectiveness of the Demand Planning process including, at a minimum, demand plan accuracy, demand plan bias, Demand Planning value-add, and parameter accuracy.

b. Demand Plan Attainment

The extent of delivering the approved monthly Aggregate Demand Plan is measured and improving.

c. Conversion of Opportunities and Vulnerabilities

Opportunities and vulnerabilities are actively managed. Identified opportunities and vulnerabilities that have been successfully exploited or mitigated are measured and improving.

d. Customer Experience

Customer experience is monitored and improving. This includes measures of how the product offering and delivery match up to customer expectations, such as net promoter score, perfect order, complaint rates, inquiry response rates.

e. Trading Partner Collaboration and Feedback

The level and effectiveness of collaboration with strategic partners are measured via feedback mechanisms; for example, 360-degree feedback is utilized.

f. Velocity

Non-value-added time in key business processes is measured and is being eliminated.

g. Market Segment Plan Performance

Delivery of the Market Segment plan in volume, revenue, and margin is measured and improving.

16. Business performance measures identify and provide focus to improve results.

a. Marketing Mix Effectiveness

Achievement of anticipated return on investment of Marketing and Sales activities is measured and improving.

b. Market Roadmap Attainment

On-time deployment of activities and achievement of planned outcomes in the Market Roadmap are measured. Gaps to achieving the Market Roadmap are identified, and gap-closure plans are developed and tracked.

c. Customer Value

Measures such as the ability to win business, customer/business retention, customer turnover, and cost-to-serve are in place and either achieving established targets or showing meaningful improvement.

7

MANAGING THE SUPPLY CHAIN

PURPOSE

To build and manage an adaptable Supply Chain and organizational capability that plans, integrates, and shapes the Supply Planning and Execution processes. The Supply Chain will deliver customer value, optimal performance aligned to the Strategic Plan, and sustainable competitive advantage.

POSITIONING

Process maturity improves over time through education, committed leadership, expert guidance, and a focused effort to attain key business milestones.

After embarking on the path to improvement, Internal and External Supply capabilities, including logistics and distribution, are routinely at a minimum of 95 percent performance. A Class A Planning and Control Milestone has been secured, positioning the business at the top of Phase 1 of Business Maturity (see Foundation, Figure I.1). Advanced Planning Systems are being deployed to provide selected Network Planning in the Supply Chain.

From this Class A Milestone vantage point, we introduce this next level of maturity in the seventh edition of *The Oliver Wight Class A Standard for Business Excellence*.

The scope for Supply Chain Management is two Nodes forward, for example, customer and consumer, and two Nodes back, supplier and supplier's supplier, including all internal processing and physical activities. Planning and Execution are integrated and optimized across adjacent Nodes of the Supply Chain, so plans and performance are optimized not just within each Node. Please note a Node is also referred to as a *Supply Point*.

Supply Chain Management will require formally agreed collaborative planning and execution between partners, with benefits shared equitably. This collaboration enables a Value Chain response. The Supply Chain will be segmented based on logic that defines and enables the operating and delivery mechanisms for service expectations, cost requirements, and cash commitment.

CHAPTER CONTENT

Driven by Strategy

Integration

Supply Chain Model

Supply Chain Planning and Synchronization

Collaboration

Data Sharing and Analytics

Network Management

Organization Design

Behavior and Competencies

Performance Measurement

DRIVEN BY STRATEGY

1. The Supply Chain Roadmap supports the Market and Product Roadmaps, delivering business and customer value.

   a. Market Roadmap and Product and Portfolio Roadmap

      The roadmaps define the required Supply Chain capability, service, and cost requirements, including where differentiated service and supply are required.

   b. Scope

      The scope of activity for the Supply Chain has been defined and clearly understood. At a minimum, this includes planning processes, physical footprint, information flow, and organization design.

   c. Supply Chain Roadmap

      This roadmap directs the Internal Supply, Network, and External Sourcing Roadmaps. They define the required capability and performance and ensure integration.

   d. Network Roadmap

      The Network Roadmap directs footprint for distribution, warehousing, operations, and routes to market in response to service levels and defines the required capability and performance.

2. The Supply Chain Model is designed to optimize service, inventory, and costs while meeting Critical Success Factors.

   a. Supply Chain Framework

      The Supply Chain Framework is defined, is understood, and includes Supply Chain characteristics: legislative, regulatory, infrastructure related, environmental, fiscal, ethical, socially responsible, geographic, political, and economic considerations. It is periodically reviewed to ensure alignment to the strategic landscape.

   b. Segmentation Considerations

      Differentiated levels of service, cost, working capital, and response determine segmentation requirements aligned to Market and Product Roadmaps.

c. Monitor for Success

There is a dynamic and systemized process in place to respond to changing conditions. Performance measures are reviewed regularly, and this drives control, root-cause analysis, and continuously improved performance.

INTEGRATION

3. **Supply Chain capability and flexibility are measured and managed through a monthly Supply Chain Review. Reconciled product, demand, and financial views are managed through Integrated Business Planning.**

a. Process Mechanism

The linkage between Supply Chain Management and other elements of Integrated Business Planning is defined and made explicit.

b. Supply Chain Integration and Linkage

Plans are received as "requirements" to the monthly Supply Planning process. Integrated Supply Plans are created, recognizing capability and flexibility within the Supply Chain. There is a collaborative approach to planning, and execution is controlled in accordance with the agreed plans.

c. Reconciliation Management

Supply Chain Management is proactive in seeking business solutions where the proposed plan implies constraint on Product Management or Demand Plans or gaps to business commitments or where risks are deemed unacceptable. The Supply Chain Review incorporates input and involves Supply Chain partners.

3. **Processes utilize real-time information for management of the collaborative Supply Chain and enable high performance to achieve Strategic Business Objectives.**

a. Demand Signal

There is clear and timely visibility of events that will change demand timing, mix, or volumes. Demand-sensing techniques are used to communicate and realign the Supply Chain partners.

b. Supply Chain Orchestration

   Visibility of Supply Chain activity is shared throughout the Supply Chain. A Supply Chain Control Tower ensures execution of plans and optimized response to change. The Control Tower is run by the Master Supply Chain Planner and is supported by integrated, real-time system information.

c. Management of Collaborative Realignment

   Trading partners have collaboratively determined exception alerts, which generate optimized realignment suggestions. These alerts and suggested changes are managed by the Control Towers to reset the Supply Chain Execution.

d. Balanced Supply Chain Performance

   Integration checkpoints have been determined through collaborative planning. These are documented in collaborative arrangements to validate that new or changed plans are on track from the Supply Chain perspective.

SUPPLY CHAIN MODEL

4. The Supply Chain Operating Model is developed to align with the strategically agreed framework and signed off by the trading partners.

a. Model Created

   The Model is created and tested based on the shared goals of the collaborative Supply Chain partners. The model uses segmentation to achieve the required levels of service, cost, and response.

b. Model Validation

   The Model has been tested against actual conditions to ensure that it best reflects the optimization rules the partners set and is reviewed frequently.

c. Ownership and Accountability

   The ownership of the Supply Chain Model is shared among key partners while the ultimate responsibility rests with the primary owner. The accountability for running and validating the Model is with the primary partner.

d. <u>Maintaining through Change</u>

The Supply Chain Team has agreed to the frequency of review of the Model, and key rules are maintained to ensure ongoing validity.

5. The Supply Chain Operating Model is the mechanism to run scenarios as the basis to optimize Supply Chain Segments.

a. <u>Footprint</u>

The Model considers the future footprint requirements based on the changing routes to market.

b. <u>Customer Value</u>

Customer value is measured and understood. The segmentation approach behind future scenarios considers the required customer value.

c. <u>Optimization Criteria Defined</u>

Optimization criteria have been agreed and are used in driving segmentation outcomes and future scenarios or decisions, including channel considerations.

d. <u>Time Fences</u>

Time fences are modeled to drive effective approaches to meeting the customers' needs while driving the required levels of Supply Chain and Operations efficiency.

6. Non-value-adding steps in the Supply Chain drive collaborative activities to improvement.

a. <u>Supply Chain Agility</u>

The requirement for Agility is understood and established in line with the Supply Chain Strategy and segments. Improvements in Agility can be demonstrated.

b. <u>Supply Chain Costs</u>

Requirements for cost reduction along the Supply Chain are understood and established in line with Supply Chain Strategy. Improvements in costs along the Supply Chain can be demonstrated.

c. Value Stream Mapping

Value Stream Mapping is regularly used to establish improvement opportunities for the Model. There is an agreed definition of value among Supply Chain partners.

d. Financial Drivers

Cost drivers in the Supply Chain are understood and agreed. There is a process for identifying value-adding and non-value-adding activity and removing waste. These drivers are managed and are an integral part of business decision making in the Supply Chain.

SUPPLY CHAIN PLANNING AND SYNCHRONIZATION

7. **The Master Supply Chain Plan synchronizes and aligns the integrated Supply Chain.**

a. Master Supply Chain Planning

The Master Supply Chain Plan is created in accordance with agreed segment parameters and optimized at the cumulative Supply Chain lead time. It is aligned to the demonstrated performance of the Supply Chain and time-phased improvement plans.

b. Integrated Plans

The concepts of Requirements Planning (using Dependent Demand) are used to manage an integrated planning process throughout the Supply Chain.

c. Resource Management

Key resources have been identified and are managed in the planning process. The planning process plans the use of capacity and capability against these resources for the entire planning horizon based on demonstrated performance concepts.

d. Integrated Planning Processes

Supply Chain Planning processes are integrated, monitored, and managed so that all aspects of inventory levels, lead times, and responsiveness meet the modeled expectations for each segment.

e. Product Management

Resource and Technology requirements to support Product Management activities have been incorporated into the Supply Chain Plan.

f. Planning Rules and Parameters

Valid planning rules maintain Supply Chain Model integrity and parameters: for example, preferred ship-from supply point, safety stock levels, lead times, etc. Ownership, change management, and integrity audits follow governance policies at a level to enable an Agile response.

8. Supply Chain Analytics and modeling techniques are used to optimize the Supply Chain and Segments.

a. Multiple Scenario Modeling

What-if scenarios determine the ability to satisfy customer demand, achieving the optimum balance for total cost and segment investment.

b. Supply Chain Optimization

Advanced Planning System techniques are used to maintain, optimize, and balance across the Supply Chain, using the rules established by the Supply Chain design.

c. Segment Optimization

Optimization choices are behind the key drivers of segmentation; actual results are measured against modeled results to ensure successful execution.

COLLABORATION

9. There is a process for selection and prioritization of collaborative partners.

a. Shared Benefits

A key criterion for partner selection is the willingness to work with shared benefits.

b. Capability

When assessing the capability of collaborative Supply Chain partners, factors including organizational maturity, market and product understanding and experience, financial stability, expertise and knowledge, and demonstrated performance are considered.

c. Sensitivity and Risk Exposure

   Risks associated with degree of dependency on a collaborative partner and with sensitivity of intellectual property and trading data are evaluated during the selection process.

d. System Infrastructure

   The compatibility and connectivity of partner planning and transactional execution systems, including capacity and transactional processing capability, are considered during the partner selection process.

10. **Collaborative agreements exist between all External Nodes in the Supply Chain. The Supply Chain is managed to these agreements.**

   a. Collaborative Agreements

      Collaborative Agreements are jointly agreed by all collaborative partners in the Supply Chain. External Node linkages are formalized through joint Business Plans and properly structured Service Level Agreements. A Change Management process exists to enable Collaborative Agreement adaptation to changing business requirements.

   b. Investment Commitment

      Investment commitments, including working capital, capital expenditure, and location to change or improve capability or capacity, are formally agreed. Joint agreements exist on inventory stocking levels and locations. The monthly Supply Chain Review is the agreed mechanism for agreeing to changes to these commitments.

   c. Levels of Authority

      Levels of authority, along with escalation criteria, are clearly defined, agreed, and documented in the Collaborative Agreements.

   d. Joint Improvement

      Collaborative goals and processes are established for Continuous Improvement. Supply Chain Key Performance Indicators (KPIs) for each segment drive waste elimination and Agility in support of the Value

Proposition, competitive advantage, and realization of shared benefits between Supply Chain partners.

e. Dispute Resolution

The mechanism for resolution of disputes between Supply Chain partners is clearly defined in the Collaborative Agreement.

f. Planning Policy and Rules

Time fence parameters have been defined for coordination and acceptable execution of change for all stages.

f. Supply Chain Performance Scorecards

The KPIs are visible through agreed scorecards and are shared with all Supply Chain partners at least monthly through a formal monthly review. Trend charts are visible and show Continuous Improvement through application of root-cause analysis and corrective actions.

DATA SHARING AND ANALYTICS

11. **A formal process for the sharing and setting of data parameters supports integrated and collaborative planning with all Supply Chain partners.**

a. Collaborative Agreements

Supply Chain Collaborative Agreements capture formal policy statements on definition, RACI (responsible, accountable, consulted, and informed), ownership, and measurement that define data-sharing models, sources of data, methods of data transmission, and confidentiality rules.

b. Data-Sharing Model and Nomenclature

Supply Chain partners jointly agree what, how, when, and with whom the data are shared. The shared data are co-owned and used to optimize plans.

c. Data Analysis

Analytics are used to enhance the performance of system alerts across the Supply Chain and support improved Supply Chain decision making. Functionality exists to enable data mining in support of optimization, exception management, scenario management, and Continuous Improvement.

d. Data Flow

Data process flows are maintained, and transmission/data format models conform to agreed definitions and industry guidelines. Real-time data flow, both dynamic and static, has been enabled.

12. **Data (including rules) used to drive the Master Supply Chain Plan are understood, accurate, and owned. They are subject to stringent change control and security governance policies.**

a. Understanding and Ownership

Users and owners of data have been educated and trained on the purpose of the data and its impact on the business.

b. Change Control Process

There is a change control process in place. Analytics identifies changes to the key Supply Chain data and evaluates the impact on the plan.

c. Data and Rules

An auditing process exists that verifies accuracy of data and rules used in the Supply Chain Model and the Master Supply Chain Plan.

d. Obsolete Data Removal

There is an Information Management procedure specifying criteria and the process for archiving obsolete master data.

NETWORK MANAGEMENT

13. **All partner Distribution and Logistics Plans are integrated with the aggregate- and detail-level Supply Chain Plans.**

a. Distribution and Logistics Optimization

Distribution and Logistics optimization considers the whole Supply Chain Network. Key Supply Chain costs, alternative transportation methods, and service and responsiveness requirements are incorporated into models to determine the optimal places to hold and consolidate inventory, points of export and import, and the optimal transportation mix.

b. Logistics Execution

A Logistics Operations and optimization process is perpetually managed to ensure a balance of stability and responsiveness. The resource deployment plan is reconciled with the monthly aggregate logistics supply plan from Integrated Business Planning. Transportation, routing schedules, and vehicle requirements are modeled at the detailed level to ensure execution optimization.

c. Integration of Network Plans

All logistics, warehousing, distribution, and transportation requirements are derived from the formal Supply Chain Plans. Inventory management decisions at the warehouse level are integrated into Demand and Supply Planning numbers.

d. Third-Party Logistics (3PL) and Procurement (3PP)

Use of outsourced logistics, manufacturing, or procurement providers has been evaluated based on the benefits associated with supporting the Supply Chain. The scope can be single or multiple Nodes.

e. Warehouse Management

The Warehouse Management system is integrated with the Master Supply Chain Plan and system over multiple time horizons. This enables changing infrastructure, resourcing, and inventory requirements to be identified, planned, and managed.

14. **The delivery process is a key requirement in achieving perfect order fulfillment and availability for use.**

a. Delivery from the Supply Chain

Delivery is organized and planned to meet the segment requirements for service, agility, and cost.

b. Distribution Networks

Where product is delivered via a Distribution Network, Distribution Resource Planning is used as the process for planning and control.

c. Transportation Optimization

Transportation optimization techniques are utilized for inbound and outbound material, including backhauls. Optimization rules reside within the Distribution Resource Planning system parameters.

d. Distribution Center Optimization

Distribution Center optimization techniques are utilized, including cross-docking and picking linearity.

e. Lean Distribution and Logistics Techniques

Lean distribution and logistics techniques are applied to warehousing, replenishment, and transportation to eliminate waste and to improve the performance of the Supply Chain in pursuit of strategy and shared benefits.

ORGANIZATION DESIGN

15. Collaborative business management throughout the Supply Chain is managed through a collaborative organizational structure.

a. Collaborative Team

The Collaborative Leadership Team includes key functions and representatives from each entity. The team defines the roles and responsibilities and sets the levels of authority.

b. Operating Team

The Operating Team manages and optimizes the model and manages the Master Supply Chain Plan. The key role of the team is to manage the Master Supply Chain Plan and model alternative options, seeking and recommending the optimized response for each segment.

BEHAVIOR AND COMPETENCIES

16. Team-based Supply Chain activities are the norm. The team includes suppliers and customers. The behaviors that define the companies' interactions have been established from become Values that enable a team-based culture and natural communication.

a. Rewards and Recognition

A team-based culture has been established, enabling both individual and team activities to be recognized and rewarded to communicate successes.

b. Ownership and Accountability

   Employees have a clear understanding and ownership of the Strategic Plan, which enables them to establish teams when deviations from the plan are detected. The use of teams is encouraged by Leadership, who hold the teams accountable through the allocation of required resources.

c. Communication

   The communication of information and data is technology enabled and has significantly reduced the need for meetings. Employees and teams naturally share their progress to accelerate learning.

d. Decisiveness

   The environment enables sharing of information and data, in real time, which are then used by employees and teams to take action.

17. **Supply Chain partners and Nodes have an established collaborative relationship that has enabled a team-based culture, with shared learning and customer focus.**

a. Collaborative

   Supply Chain partners operate as part of the Supply Chain Team. They work toward common goals and take ownership of the Supply Chain Model, Master Plans, and Supply Chain measures.

b. Customer Focus

   For each segment, the Supply Chain Team focuses on delivering value to the end customers or consumers. There is a clear understanding of the role of each Supply Chain partner in achieving this.

c. Cultural Awareness

   Supply Chain partners and team members understand and respect the values of their external partners. Alignment of organizations to a common set of values and operating principles is understood. Trust is demonstrated through joint Strategic and Business Plans, sharing and guarding confidential data and intellectual property.

d. Learning

   Continuous learning is valued and managed explicitly by the Collaborative Team. Focus areas include collaboration, system integration analytics and modeling, and a combined approach to driving Continuous Improvement. The Supply Chain Team teaches the required skills to new employees or new Supply Chain Nodes.

18. **Competencies are unique skills, talents, and proficiencies to ensure individual, team, and organizational success. Competencies are developed to support current and future needs, in both development and delivery.**

   a. Leadership

   The Leadership Team has the vision to integrate the capabilities of the Supply Chain to deliver the Strategic Business Objectives.

   b. Design

   This is the ability to analyze and configure the segmented Supply Chain Network and organization to support Market Segments and satisfy regulatory requirements.

   c. Planning and Execution

   This is the ability to apply appropriate technology to ensure information sharing and collaboration to optimize Supply Chain Planning and execution.

PERFORMANCE MEASUREMENT

19. **A balanced hierarchy of measures exists to manage and improve processes and performance in the Supply Chain. All measures have ownership and accountability and are integrated as part of the collaborative suite to drive improvement.**

   a. Balanced Set

   A balanced set of measures used in the Supply Chain supports the Model's optimized outcome. The collaboration partners understand that the overall Supply Chain delivery performance is the product of the performance of each step.

   b. Benchmarking

   Benchmarking of comparable Supply Chains is regarded as an excellent source for performance improvement opportunity. It is a routine activity.

c. Integrated Suite

Conflict between measures has been eliminated through the setting of collaborative strategic priorities. The Measurement Hierarchy demonstrating the linkage between Nodes is understood and aligned. Measures that promote Supply Chain thinking rather than functional behaviors are utlized.

d. Ownership and Accountability

All the partners in the Supply Chain have agreed on a common definition for service level measures. Overall Supply Chain service performance measures are visible at all supply points and are co-owned.

e. Goal Driven to Strategic Business Objectives

Individuals and teams in the Supply Chain have clear goals and targets linked to the Strategic Business Objectives of the business.

20. **Process measures have been defined within the hierarchy. These monitor the performance of key processes that enable Supply Chain performance. The specifics of these Key Performance Indicators will vary based on the Strategic Plan and Collaborative Agreements. Targets have been set, and improvements are being achieved.**

a. Performance to Plan

Achievement of the Supply Chain Plans approved by the Integrated Business Planning process is measured. Gaps to established targets are subject to corrective action, and improvement plans are monitored.

b. Perfect Order

The concept of the Perfect Order is understood and defined. The Supply Chain measures Perfect Order performance to identify Supply Chain opportunities to improve the customer experience.

c. Lead-Time Performance

Lead time is the length of time allowed in the planning system from the start to finish of a process. Each Node, and the entire Supply Chain, reflects lead-time reality, and measures demonstrate that lead time is reducing.

d. Velocity Ratio

The added-value time as a ratio of total elapsed time, for each step and for the entire Supply Chain, is measured and improving.

e. Inventory Turns

   Inventory turns are measured across the Supply Chain. Detail includes the
Internal and the External Nodes involving collaborative partners. Inventory
performance relative to established targets is measured, gaps are identified, and
improvement programs are put into place.

21. **Business performance measures are defined in the Business Scorecard. The specifics
of these Key Performance Indicators will vary based on the Strategic Plan and
Collaborative Agreements. Targets have been set, and improvements are being
achieved.**

a. Cash to Cash

   The Cash Conversion Cycle (CCC) considers all steps in the Supply Chain.
Measurement of CCC is used to drive competitive priorities and the selection of
sustainable partnerships.

b. Customer Service

   On-time delivery to first request: Delivery In Full On Time (DIFOT) at every
step is measured and is improving.

c. Cost Reduction to Plan

   Cost reduction is recognized as necessary to the overall health of each step in
the Supply Chain. Through cost reduction measurement, partners gain insights
into the resources or investment needed for capability improvement.

d. Margin Improvement to Plan

   Margin improvement is measured throughout the Supply Chain. Formal
agreements support improvement through direct collaborative sharing of
value creation and benefits.

8

MANAGING INTERNAL SUPPLY

PURPOSE

To support the Strategic Plan through the optimization of Internal Supply planning and execution capabilities. Internal Supply will deliver customer value, routinely deliver financial goals, and maintain performance to Class A expectations.

POSITIONING

The Internal Supply Roadmap is derived from the Supply Chain Roadmap and is used to enable a world-class Supply Chain response that delivers value to customers and consumers as part of an overall Value Chain. Internal Supply includes all aspects of planning and execution to manage the company's supply and delivery capability to guarantee customer value. The key disciplines involved are Master and Advanced Planning; Material and Capacity Planning, Inventory Management, and Planned Preventive Maintenance (PPM).

Process maturity improves over time through education, committed leadership, expert guidance, and a focused effort to attain key business milestones.

After embarking on the path to improvement, accountabilities are assigned, the elements and characteristics of the processes are implemented, and targeted measures drive improvement to enable process transformation.

Done well, a Class A Milestone is achieved at the top of Phase 1 of Business Maturity (see Foundation, Figure I.1). At this stage, Internal Supply capabilities enable valid plans routinely executed to 95 percent performance, coordination across the business to maintain one set of numbers, clarity on constraints, and a Supply Model managed through effective use of Enterprise Resource Planning (ERP) systems. Culture is addressed through an educated workforce driving values of openness and honesty, with ownership and accountability.

From this Class A Milestone vantage point, we introduce the next level of maturity in the seventh edition of *The Oliver Wight Class A Standard for Business Excellence.*

In this chapter, we discuss *Supply Points*, which can also be referred to as *Nodes.*

CHAPTER CONTENT

Driven by Strategy

Integration

Internal Supply Planning

Supply Execution

Internal Supply Modeling

Driving Internal Supply Improvements

Acquisitions, Use and Care of Assets, and Working Environment

Behaviors and Competencies

Performance Measurement

DRIVEN BY STRATEGY

1. The Supply Chain Roadmap is used to develop the Internal Supply Roadmap, which defines the Value Proposition and segmented supply response.

a. Alignment to Strategic Business Objectives

The role, purpose, and focus of each Supply Point are defined, and objectives have been set to optimize the Supply Chain. Each Supply Point can demonstrate an understanding of how its role fits with the Supply Chain and the Supply Chain Roadmap. Priorities are clearly understood, communicated, and tracked.

b. Impact of the Roadmap Is Understood

The trade-offs for delivering the Supply Point's Roadmap have been optimized in consideration of risk, investment, capability, and capacity. Competing objectives throughout the Supply Chain have been identified and reconciled. Core competencies and capabilities are defined, and gaps are addressed in the roadmap.

c. Ability to Deliver the Roadmap

Internal Supply has assessed its process and people capabilities to deliver the segmented supply response to the roadmap. Critical Success Factors to delivering the roadmap have been clearly defined with regard to timing and urgency.

2. The Internal Supply Roadmap drives the development of the Supply Model, which integrates the necessary activities to deliver the Supply Chain Roadmap and customer expectations.

a. Supply Objectives

A Supply Model has been developed and sets the assumptions for Supply Planning and Execution. It includes plans and requirements to deliver a segmented supply response, which considers inventory, agility, velocity, quality, and cost. Constraints and risks within the Model are understood and mitigated where required.

b. Agility

The level of cost-effective Agility required by the Internal Supply Roadmap to meet short- and mid-term variation in demands is made explicit within the Supply Model, and drivers are understood. Reliance on hedging is optimized by understanding the root causes and ongoing deployment of improvement plans.

c. Customer and Consumer Value Satisfied

There is an understanding of what provides value to customers and consumers. Value drives actions and improvements.

INTEGRATION

3. Internal Supply capability and flexibility are modeled, measured, and optimized as part of a monthly Supply Chain Review process. Integration with Product Management, Demand, and Financial Planning is through Integrated Business Planning.

a. Process Mechanism

Linkages between Internal Supply and other elements in the Integrated Business Planning process are defined. Synchronized supply plans are created, recognizing capability and flexibility within the Supply Chain.

b. Linkage to Product and Portfolio Management and Demand

Plans are received from Product and Portfolio Management and from Demand as "requirements" to the Supply Planning process.

c. Linkage within the Supply Chain

The signals from Internal or External Supply Points are effective. Supply Points understand their roles and responsibilities within the Supply Chain.

d. Linkage to Financial Planning

The Financial Planning process utilizes the latest Supply Chain Plans, including planned cost reduction, improvement actions, and financial projections. Finance is integral to the validation team for Business Improvement actions.

e. Integration and Optimization Management

In conjunction with External Supply or Supply Chain, Internal Supply is proactive in seeking business solutions where the proposed plan implies constraint to Product and Portfolio or Demand Management plans. Gaps to business commitments, or where risks are deemed unacceptable, are determined and adjustments made in the Integration and Optimization process or at the Management Business Review based on recommendations.

f. Linkage to People Operations

People Operations act as a business partner to Internal Supply management to ensure that the behaviors and competencies required to achieve the Internal Supply Plans are being developed.

g. Linkage to Business Improvement

Progress in Business Improvement activities associated with Internal Supply is reviewed at the monthly Supply Chain Review.

4. Internal Supply has process-based linkages with adjacent Supply Points to optimize roadmap and segmentation responses across the Supply Chain.

a. Scope of the Supply Point

The Supply Point's inputs, outputs, and process responsibilities are clearly defined. Planning parameters and rules are clear. Enabling automation is applied where value is added. The Supply Chain Roadmap is consistently being supported and challenged to drive improvement.

b. Interface with the External Supply Chain

Supply Chain links have been modeled and utilized to evaluate the impact of uncertainty and risk. The value and purpose of process steps are clearly understood. Process-Based partnerships and Collaborative Agreements exist with customers and suppliers.

c. Interfacing within the Internal Supply Point

Processes for interfacing between steps in the Supply Chain are effective and enable change to be proactively and effectively managed, resulting in Supply Chain Agility. Within these processes, problem resolution and performance reviews are clearly defined, and improvements are being demonstrated. Process-Based Teams have replaced the functional organization.

d. Gaps Are Identified and Are Explicit

Gaps between the supply plan and roadmap are visible, and there are processes to reconcile their differences. Financially analyzed options and recommendations to close gaps are routinely developed for Internal Supply and Supply Chain Team approval. Escalation is by exception.

e. Process Is Enabled by Application of Technology

Business Excellence is understood. Opportunities to improve the quality and speed of information transfer are applied. Enabling tools are deployed and used to drive improvements above the current level of performance.

INTERNAL SUPPLY PLANNING

5. Master Supply Planning has evolved to include Advanced Planning techniques. Master Supply Planning is Knowledge Based, and that knowledge is embedded in technology.

a. The Supply Planner

The key role of the Supply Planner is to develop opportunities and improvements to deliver the Internal Supply Roadmap. The Supply Planner is accountable for the rule-based Supply Plan.

b. Plans

The Supply Plan is aligned to the Internal Supply Roadmap to provide a segmented supply response. It demonstrates the required capability and agility with a financial and operational view of planned activities.

c. Translation of Plans

There is clear alignment across all planning horizons, which are customer focused, are integrated, and use appropriate management and planning techniques.

d. Resource Planning

Critical resources are managed, and goals are set to optimize those resources, both internally and externally.

e. Systems, Tools, and Data

There is a seamless suite of tools to provide rule-based automation of the Supply Plan. The knowledge behind the plan is managed, maintained, and improved by the Supply Planner. There is tool-based integration with adjacent Supply Points.

f. Planning and Scheduling Techniques

The Supply Model provides clear direction on appropriate planning and scheduling techniques using the planning parameters, available capacity, and agility requirements/capabilities.

g. Linkages to the Master Supply Schedule

The Internal Supply Plan is managed at the appropriate level of granularity over the entire planning horizon. Time zones within the planning horizon are segment/ product specific and enable planned agility.

6. **The impact of Agility on Internal Supply is understood, is modeled, and provides a cost-effective and planned response to anticipated and unanticipated demands.**

a. Agility Planning

The requirement for Agility is known, planned, and modeled through the planning horizon. Constraints and improvements are resolved through Integrated Business Planning. There is a commitment to maintaining Agility as a competitive advantage.

b. Agility Execution

The short-term utilization of Agility is measured. The amount of unutilized Agility is known, is stated as an opportunity, and is appropriately utilized.

c. Cost of Agility

The cost of planning and utilizing Agility is known and modeled.

d. Lean

The process of deriving Agility is initially from existing resources. Where resources have been exhausted, resources are added in line with the Internal Supply Roadmap.

SUPPLY EXECUTION

7. **Processes ensure a commitment to execute the schedule.**

a. Deliver the Schedule

An automated order release occurs at least daily, with the Process Team demonstrating schedule adherence, consistently achieving a minimum performance of Four Sigma.

b. Documentation

The execution process is fully documented, and simplification is evident due to the automation of routine execution tasks.

c. Supplier Scheduling

Simplification of the execution tasks to add Value and Agility is evident. Use of supplier scheduling or pull techniques is the norm. Supplier delivery performance is measured and achieves a minimum of Four Sigma. Where pull techniques are used, the number of Kanban violations is less than 0.5 percent.

8. **Competitive advantage is enabled through sustainable Velocity improvement and Agile response.**

a. Execution Communication

Communication is two-way, automated, and provided by systematic mechanisms. The release horizon is being reduced.

b. Process Flow

Demand push and pull mechanisms are deployed, and applicable techniques are used to control flow of material. All techniques have specific documented operating rules, which are rigorously adhered to. Batch and queue sizes are reducing and challenged routinely to determine whether they meet current or near-term business conditions and drive improvement.

c. Velocity

The Velocity Ratio is measured and reported. Value Stream Mapping is employed to identify opportunities for improvement, resulting in reductions in lot sizes and lead times. There is a stable increase in inventory turns.

d. Waste Elimination Culture and Behavior

The elimination of waste from business processes is a stated objective, and there is an active and visible program to empower people and teams to identify and eliminate waste. Balanced efficiency measures are used to improve Supply Chain performance.

e. Agility

Agility is viewed as a competitive advantage and is proactively managed and incorporated into the supply plans. The key drivers of Agility are lead-time reductions, batch-size reduction, change-over improvement, and asset flexibility and are actively leveraged in the supply plans.

INTERNAL SUPPLY MODELING

9. Data and their rules are enablers of modeling and automation.

a. <u>Data Accuracy</u>

Data accuracy is maintained at a Four Sigma level and represents no additional cost to the business, as it is achieved through Lean principles and automation.

b. <u>Dynamic Data</u>

Transactions are completed in real time and error proofed.

c. <u>Rules</u>

Rule-based automation, where used, is supported by demonstrated best practices and links directly to the Supply Model.

d. <u>Governance Process</u>

A governance process drives the introduction, expansion, and obsolescence of data sets used in the Internal Supply Planning process. Rules governing data use are documented and audited.

e. <u>Organization Evolved</u>

The ownership of data has migrated to the point of use. The role of centralized data management has evolved to governance and analytics.

10. The Internal Supply response to changing business and segmentation requirements is dynamically modeled to identify opportunities.

a. <u>Characteristics</u>

The Internal Supply Models are owned by the Supply Planner. Data for modeling are easily and quickly available. The confidence level of models is known throughout the planning horizon. Constraints and risks within the models are reviewed through the Integrated Business Planning process.

b. <u>Internal Supply Point Modeling</u>

The Internal Supply Point is modeled using multiple inputs that contribute to the understanding of cost, service, risk, and agility of resulting plans.

c. Internal Supply Point Contribution to Supply Chain Modeling (Segmentation, Agility, and Risk)

The Internal Supply Point contributes to the Supply Chain Model and provides a segmented supply response in line with the Supply Chain Roadmap. The Agility required by this roadmap and associated risks are explicit.

d. Analytics

Analytics and predictive modeling are being used to drive greater understanding, create scenarios, and enable decision making.

e. Role of Supply Analyst

The Supply Analyst is a senior member of the Supply Chain Team who provides the Supply Chain ongoing visibility and insight into macro and micro process trends, customer and supplier insights, and competitive intelligence.

DRIVING INTERNAL SUPPLY IMPROVEMENTS

11. **Governance is achieved through Integrated Business Planning to ensure strategic alignment and compliance of improvement activities with company ethics and values.**

a. Prioritization of Improvement

Where improvement initiatives have been identified and supported with a clear business case, and there is a conflict over resource availability, a governance structure exists to prioritize and filter. The two-job culture is a way of life throughout the organization, and people understand their decision rights.

b. Legislation and Regulatory Requirements

The Internal Supply Team has the required knowledge of current legislation and regulatory requirements, which are incorporated into current plans. These plans are then adjusted as future changes are identified and confirmed through the Supply Chain Roadmap. Proactive involvement with regulatory agencies is leveraged for enhanced consumer safety and barriers to a competitor's Supply Chain.

c. Quality

The full scope of quality needs is a way of life and reflected in all activities, plans, and improvements.

d. Ethics and Values

    There are clear company statements around ethics and values that everybody in the organization understands and consistently applies.

e. Policies and Documentation

    Migration from paper documentation and policies to electronically controlled execution and compliance with the process has taken place.

12. A clear leadership expectation motivates the organization to identify opportunities for improvement where appropriate tools are deployed to support the requirements of the roadmaps. A knowledgeable work force owns the strategic direction and drives improvement.

a. Education and Training

    Internal education and training programs incorporate the latest knowledge and skill to ensure that the latest best practice is shared formally and in an appropriate manner.

b. Ideation and Innovation

    Processes have been established to regularly collect, prioritize, and select ideas for improvement that could lead to innovations that will step change the organization's capability.

c. Lean and Six Sigma

    There is a common understanding of Lean principles and a relentless pursuit of waste elimination throughout the business. Through the reduction of waste and realignment of value-added steps, the overall Velocity is significantly improved to Class A levels of performance.

d. Planned Agility

    Improvements in process velocity enable Internal Supply to commit to cost-effective Agility for anticipated variation in customer demands. When executing this capability, the released schedules are unaffected.

e. Linkage to Measurement Hierarchy

    The visibility provided through the Measurement Hierarchy of gaps or areas requiring improvement activity is used to drive ideation and innovation processes.

ACQUISITIONS, USE AND CARE OF ASSETS, AND WORKING ENVIRONMENT

13. Equipment and asset utilization plans are supportive of the Internal Supply Roadmap and planned Agility. The organization drives improvements in asset and equipment effectiveness, which creates the visibility for future acquisitions and investments. The ergonomics of the working environment are regularly reviewed to optimize flow and well-being.

a. Acquisition

Total Cost of Ownership in support of roadmaps is the basis for acquisition of assets, and approval is via the Integrated Business Planning process. The overall acquisition process includes acquisition, installation, training, and commissioning, all of which are planned and integrated into the Internal Supply Planning process.

b. Overall Equipment Effectiveness (OEE) and Technically, Environmentally, and Economically Practicable (TEEP)

The desire to utilize assets 100 percent has been modified to align with scheduled requirements. However, equipment needs to be production ready and deliver demonstrated capability. There is an agreed balance between the need for Agility and response to normal variation in demands with a desire to minimize any increase to the cost per unit.

c. Ergonomics

Ownership of the workplace has been established with the Process Team, and ongoing investment is available to improve the ergonomics such that workflows are optimal. Having established workplace ownership, the Process Team is empowered to improve their own working environments.

d. Predictive Maintenance

Planned Preventive Maintenance is focused on Predictive Maintenance. All maintenance activities are scheduled and measured, providing greater insight and understanding for potential investments and acquisitions decisions.

BEHAVIORS AND COMPETENCIES

14. Expressed behaviors, supporting the Business Values, define the company interactions and responses. An environment exists that encourages expert teams who are motivated to accept empowerment and take initiative.

a. <u>Rewards and Recognition</u>

Individuals and teams are recognized for their contribution, and team success has become the focus.

b. <u>Ownership and Accountability</u>

Individuals and teams have the confidence to make decisions and are held accountable. Potential failure is mitigated through team ownership. Sponsorship is demonstrated by the Leadership Team.

c. <u>Communication</u>

Communication is a priority, is continuous, is reinforced, and is appropriate to the target audience to ensure company-wide understanding.

d. <u>Decisiveness</u>

In the face of uncertainty, decision making is accelerated because of clear lines of authority. Roles and responsibilities and associated decision rights are regularly redefined to broaden their scope in response to organization changes.

e. <u>Style and Leadership for Change</u>

The Leadership Team actively encourage a culture of change and empower individuals and teams to drive improvements. The Leadership Team has a leadership style that supports an empowered organization and enables Situational Leadership to be deployed.

f. <u>Teams</u>

Natural teams drive business processes. Self-directed teams are starting to evolve. Process-based thinking has become a way of life.

g. <u>Culture</u>

A nurturing and inclusive culture of empowerment exists at all levels to create shared understanding. The organization values diversity, but decisions are based on consensus. Trust has been earned up and down the organization.

h. Intelligent Processes

Knowledge is captured in the process, which becomes intuitive and self-sustaining and enables flexibility and progression.

15. **Competencies are unique skills, talents, and proficiencies to ensure individual, team, and organizational success. The organization structure has evolved to enable behaviors, teamwork, and decision rights that align to the Internal Supply Chain Roadmap.**

a. Planning

Product, process, and technology knowledge develop predictive models used to optimize plans.

b. Execution

Application of Lean, Velocity, and Agile techniques enables flawless execution.

c. Customer Focus

There is a passion for customer success based on an understanding of customers' requirements. The organizational structure enables collaboration through a Bow Tie to Diamond evolution.

d. Structure

The organization has evolved to a broader, flatter structure, which provides a responsive and agile capability with greatly simplified communication through fewer layers.

e. Management of the Virtual Organization

The capability to manage a virtual organization increases as the structure changes in response to new challenges and collaboration.

PERFORMANCE MEASUREMENT

16. **A balanced hierarchy of key measures with targets and time-phased improvement has been defined by the supply organization. These measures are critical drivers of competitive advantage and delivery of the Supply Chain Roadmap.**

a. Measures Defined and Understood

A balanced suite of measures has been defined, and targets are based on external benchmarking where possible and support achievement of the Supply

Chain Roadmap. The measures have been communicated to all stakeholders and supply teams.

b. Reviewed

The key measures are regularly reviewed to align Supply Management activities to the Supply Chain Roadmap and achievement of Critical Success Factors. Key Performance Indicators and targets are changed to maintain visibility and prioritize improvement.

c. Hierarchical Linkage

There is a clear hierarchical link between the suite of key measures for each business process and the Business Scorecard. Once process proficiency has been established, the measures are delegated and redefined, or the targets are revised.

d. Competitive Advantage

Measures, and associated Key Performance Indicators, are seen as a competitive advantage, not just goals to be achieved; consequently, measures drive individual and team-based behaviors.

e. Balance

A reasonable balance of measures exists across process areas.

f. Evolving

It is recognized that when percentile performance is insufficient to determine improvements, a migration to Six Sigma methodology/statistical performances is required.

17. **Process measures are valued by the Internal Supply organization to drive and demonstrate delivery of the roadmaps. Process measures are agreed in advance to ensure Class A performance.**

a. Suite of Process Measures

There is a suite of measures for efficiency, agility, velocity, and capability covering the full scope of Internal Supply.

b. Perfect Order

The concept of the Perfect Order is understood and defined for the company. The Internal Supply organization measures Perfect Order performance to identify Supply Management opportunities to improve the customer experience.

c. People

People-related measures are used to identify team and individual contributions to Internal Supply deliverables. Opportunities for improvement are identified, plans are put into place, and results are measured.

18. **Business performance measures are established in recognition that process measures alone are insufficient. Business performance measures are agreed in advance to ensure Class A performance and ensure Value to stakeholders.**

a. Strategic Alignment

Strategic Plan alignment is confirmed through the Critical Success Factors Roadmap.

b. Financial

Financial success is confirmed through plan attainment and is monitored through Integrated Business Planning.

c. Variance to Plan

Variance to plan is understood in both financial and operational performance terms.

d. Customer Service

On-time delivery to first request: Delivery In Full On Time (DIFOT) at every step, from Internal Supply to the customer, is measured and is improving.

e. Inventory

Inventory turns based on modeled targets and benchmarks are measured across the Internal Supply Chain. Inventory performance relative to established targets is measured, gaps are identified, and improvement programs are put into place.

9

MANAGING EXTERNAL SOURCING

PURPOSE

To support the Strategic Plan by sourcing and managing the incoming supply of goods and services to competitive advantage, ensuring Class A Supply Chain performance. To understand and manage the balance between risk and Total Cost of Ownership.

POSITIONING

The External Sourcing Roadmap is derived directly from the Supply Chain Roadmap. It establishes the required supplier base and relationships to enable a world-class Supply Chain response that delivers value to customers and consumers as part of an overall Value Chain. The roadmap drives the integration of processes to ensure Supply Chain Plans manage supplier responses. The processes involved are creations of externally sourced categories, supplier selection and collaboration, and Total Cost of Ownership. The roadmap will identify the required agility from suppliers, in support of supply chain performance and product development collaboration.

Process maturity improves over time through education, committed leadership, expert guidance, and a focused effort to attain key business milestones.

After embarking on the path to improvement, accountabilities are assigned, the elements and characteristics of the processes are implemented, and targeted measures drive improvement to enable process transformation.

Done well, a Class A Milestone is achieved at the top of Phase 1 of Business Maturity (see Foundation, Figure I.1). At this stage, formal make/buy processes are deployed, Supplier Capability Reviews drive performance, routinely executed to 95 percent, from a rationalized supplier base, and the business has introduced Total Cost of Ownership.

129

From this Class A Milestone vantage point, we introduce the next level of maturity in the seventh edition of *The Oliver Wight Class A Standard for Business Excellence.*

CHAPTER CONTENT

Driven by Strategy

Integration

External Sourcing Roadmap

Total Cost of Ownership

Continuity of Supply

Supplier Analysis, Selection, and Business Agreements

Supplier Relationships

Behaviors and Competencies

Performance Measurement

DRIVEN BY STRATEGY

1. **The Strategic Plan includes Market, Product and Portfolio, Supply Chain, and Finance Roadmaps. These have been used to develop the External Sourcing Roadmap.**

   a. Documented Roadmap

   A Sourcing Roadmap exists that defines those items or services that, for strategic reasons, the company has defined to be internally sourced. For all other items or services, potential external sources of supply are evaluated with internal sourcing options to support a formal make/buy process.

   b. Review Process

   The Sourcing Roadmap is reviewed regularly to ensure that it is congruent with the overall Strategic Plan and that it meets current business needs, as circumstances change internally and externally.

   c. Roadmap Review

   Development of the Sourcing Roadmap is a team activity. Recommendations and decisions are reviewed and agreed through Integrated Business Planning.

   d. Comparison of Benefits

   Total Cost of Ownership is used for the valid comparison of costs and benefits between internal and external sources of supply. The comparison is conducted by an independent function, generally but not exclusively Finance.

2. **The business recognizes the key role of External Sourcing and prioritizes business resources to support high-value-adding activities, generated from external sources, which are aligned with the future strategic development of the business.**

   a. Innovation

   There is a formal business process to enable supplier innovation. There is clear accountability for External Sourcing to proactively seek new Core Competencies at external sources of supply.

   b. Core Competencies

   The potential strategic benefits of new Core Competencies within the supplier base are fully evaluated in the external and internal sourcing decision-making process.

c. Make/Buy Decisions

The formal, multi-functional process for make/buy decisions includes an understanding of potential consequences to the supplier base. Any resulting risk to the internal business is identified with suitable risk mitigation as part of the business case. It fully evaluates all internal or external investment requirements.

d. Review Process

There is a formal governance and review process such that actual costs and benefits of the make/buy decisions are calculated and measured against the original estimates to gauge how successful the decision-making process has been and to learn for the future.

INTEGRATION

3. **External supply capability and flexibility are modeled, measured, and optimized through the monthly Supply Chain Review process. Integration with Product Management, Demand Management, and Financial Planning is ensured through Integrated Business Planning.**

a. Process Mechanism

The linkage between External Supply and the core processes in Integrated Business Planning is defined and made explicit, irrespective of whether this is an integrated business unit or a stand-alone activity in a multi-entity organization. External capability and risk are given equal importance in the process.

b. Linkage to Product Management

Plans received from Product Management for the introduction of new and modified products and services, and product and service discontinuation, take full account of supplier capabilities and commitments made. This includes the implications of integrating new core competencies within the supplier base.

c. Linkage to Specification Management

Specification creation and Change Management processes are integrated with supplier technical authorities where appropriate, and timely reviews and approvals take place in collaboration with the supply base.

d. Linkage to Integration and Optimization

External Sourcing is proactive in developing business solutions where the proposed plan implies constraints to Product or Supply Chain Plans, gaps to business commitments, or unacceptable risks. Adjustments made via the Integration and Optimization processor, the Management Business Review, are applied to revised External Sourcing Plans.

e. Linkage to People Operations

People Operations act as a business partner to External Sourcing and ensure that behaviors and competencies required to achieve the External Supply Plans are being planned and developed.

f. Linkage to Business Improvement

Progress in Business Improvement activities associated with External Sourcing is reviewed at the monthly Supply Chain Review.

4. **Suppliers' capabilities in terms of capacity, quality, responsiveness, and technology are managed as crucial elements of the Supply Chain Operating Model.**

a. Supply Planning

Suppliers' capabilities and potential constraints are understood and regularly reviewed at the Supplier Capability Review and are inputs to the Supply Chain Operating Model.

b. Supplier Initiatives

Key supplier initiatives affecting their capability are similarly reviewed at the Supplier Capability Review, and changes become inputs to the Supply Chain Operating Model.

c. Supplier Quality

Supplier quality audits take place according to predetermined criteria before supplier approval. Supplier quality processes and improvement programs are monitored and reported to ensure integration with the company's quality systems.

d. Technological Capability

There is a process to ensure that suppliers' technological capability matches the company's proposed future Product Portfolio Plan.

e. Ethical Considerations

There is a process to ensure appointed suppliers demonstrate ethical practices aligned with the company's strategic direction on corporate responsibility (ethical sourcing, sustainability, customer due diligence).

EXTERNAL SOURCING ROADMAP

5. The External Sourcing Roadmap supports the Supply Chain Roadmap and drives Procurement activities.

a. Company Values

The External Sourcing Roadmap and activities are underpinned by the company Values. These are well understood by the Procurement Team.

b. Review Process

A process exists to periodically review progress and evolution of the documented External Sourcing Roadmap to ensure alignment with the Strategic Plan and Value Proposition.

c. E-Procurement Roadmap

The company has a clearly defined e-procurement component of its Information Technology Roadmap, which drives automation, collaborative planning and sourcing and, where appropriate, e-portal platform to share data and information. This is based on the commodity group profile and supplier tier structure.

d. Alternative Supply Channels

The company continuously evaluates opportunities with alternative sources of supply, considering such factors as geography, industry, and regulations, to create competitive advantage.

6. Externally sourced materials and services are combined into logical groups, such as commodities and categories, and a clear External Sourcing Roadmap is defined for each.

a. Commodity Groupings

Commodity groupings have been agreed and documented.

b. Commodity Group Allocation

All externally sourced materials and services (including intra-company where appropriate) have been allocated a commodity group.

c. Commodity Group Profiling

Commodity group profiling is carried out regularly, considering factors such as cost, risk, technology, vulnerability, and strategic significance.

d. Commodity Group Acquisition Strategy

There is a formal process to agree on the acquisition strategy for each commodity group, based on the company spend profile and supplier capabilities. It considers marketplace characteristics, geographic supply capabilities, quality, service, capacity, and total cost of ownership.

e. Single versus Multi-Source

A formal risk analysis is carried out for those materials and services where supply availability is vulnerable. Single or multi-sourcing policies are aligned to this. The risk analysis is refreshed periodically and is reviewed for changes in market dynamics as well as supplier capability.

TOTAL COST OF OWNERSHIP

7. **Total Cost of Ownership is recognized as the decision-making tool for assessing competing suppliers in making sourcing decisions.**

a. Assessment

Total Cost of Ownership is the key tool for Internal and External Strategic Sourcing decisions.

b. Procurement Measurement

Total Cost of Ownership is the tool used to measure the effectiveness of External Sourcing.

c. Traditional Measures

Traditional performance measures have been replaced by Total Cost of Ownership where appropriate and practical.

d. Multi-Functional Participation

> The template for each commodity group has been agreed by all interested functions, including Finance.

8. A Total Cost of Ownership analysis is in place to consistently calculate lifetime costs for all key materials, goods, and services.

a. Template

> The Total Cost of Ownership template considers the present value of all costs that will be incurred over the life of the product or service.

b. Inclusion of All Costs

> The template includes all aspects of the lifetime total cost. This includes not only price but also factors such as transportation costs, quality costs, on-time delivery performance, inventory holding, response times from the supplier, projected exchange rate fluctuations, processing costs, servicing and maintenance costs, resale value, depreciation, and disposal costs.

c. Commodity Group Profiling

> The Total Cost of Ownership template is developed for each commodity grouping used in commodity group profiling.

d. Periodic Reviews

> Templates are regularly reviewed to ensure validity. Changes in key variables, such as currency exchange rates and interest rates, are captured.

e. Interim and Final Reviews

> Periodically, and at the end of life for the material or service used, the actual total cost is compared to the original calculation. This comparison is used to aid future learning.

f. Should Cost

> For key categories, should-cost models will be in evidence to ensure appropriate cost targets and negotiation leverage.

CONTINUITY OF SUPPLY

9. The complete Supply Chain for all strategically significant, externally sourced materials and services is fully documented and managed.

a. Documentation

   The Supply Chain for all strategically significant products and services is mapped; constraints, risks, and contingency measures are identified.

b. First-Tier Suppliers

   A category review takes place to ensure the responsibilities of first-tier suppliers, in terms of managing their own supplier base, are appropriate.

c. Second- and Third-Tier Suppliers

   When required, second- and third-tier suppliers are also reviewed for long-term capability in the same way as first-tier suppliers.

d. End Use and Consumption

   Future changes in end-user markets are understood and documented to evaluate vulnerabilities and opportunities to the incoming Supply Chain.

e. Supplier Quality Management

   A formal process and operating model exists to ensure supplier quality is audited, measured, and analyzed by an independent, qualified part of the organization. Key suppliers are encouraged to self-assess and act upon findings autonomously. Cost of poor quality is understood and is part of Total Cost Management.

10. Analytical methods are used to minimize risk to the company by ensuring the continuity of externally sourced materials and services.

a. Risk Analysis

   Risk studies are carried out on all key suppliers, using appropriate analysis tools.

b. Supplier Financial and Business Performance

   Key financial ratios and business performance for all major and strategically significant second- and third-tier suppliers are regularly reviewed.

c. Supplier Internal Systems

   Suppliers' internal processes and systems are reviewed to ensure that they are sufficient to support company requirements.

d. Disaster Recovery Planning

   There is a disaster recovery plan in place for all commodities and suppliers where the company is vulnerable. These plans are regularly reviewed and updated.

SUPPLIER ANALYSIS, SELECTION, AND BUSINESS AGREEMENTS

11. There is a structured supplier evaluation and selection process for each commodity that considers all relevant requirements.

a. Multi-Functional Involvement

   The evaluation and selection of suppliers is a multi-functional activity, facilitated by External Sourcing.

b. Breadth of Process

   The process considers, where appropriate, manufacturing, quality systems, service support, health, safety, environment, new product development, ethical considerations, and other relevant business processes. It ensures sourcing will not compromise company values.

c. Financial Viability

   Supplier financial viability is considered part of the selection process.

d. Parent Company Relationship

   Where the supplier is part of a larger group, the parent company's relationship in terms of meeting the defined requirements and ensuring continuity of supply is considered. The supplier's strategic significance to the parent company is also evaluated.

e. Capacity Constraints

   Supplier key capacity constraints are understood and used by Master Supply Planning.

f. Transparency of Decision Making

   The reasons for supplier selection are fully understood and documented.

12. Collaborative agreements are drawn up with key suppliers, appropriate to the nature of the supply. Formal agreements remain with all other suppliers.

a. Collaborative Agreements

Collaborative agreements exist with key suppliers to capture the shared working relationship in support of the Supply Chain Roadmap.

b. Business Agreement Structure

The Business Agreement describes how business will be conducted and monitored and includes items such as standards of behavior, ethics, communication channels, time fences, flexibility of supply, review processes, joint projects, and technology support.

c. Performance Levels

The Business Agreement will specify agreed performance levels, measures, and continuous improvement activities.

d. New Suppliers

For new suppliers, there is a clear process for communicating the company organization structure, business processes, and values.

e. Review Process

There is a review process for the business agreement itself, and the review takes place at least annually.

SUPPLIER RELATIONSHIPS

13. The company is committed to a supplier development program and collaborative planning to sustain long-term Supply Chain improvement objectives.

a. Supplier Collaboration Roadmap

The roadmap is determined with formal guidelines, allowing differentiation based on the marketplace and the criticality of the category. Roles and responsibilities are understood.

b. Transfer of Information and Collaborative Planning

A process ensures the two-way transfer of collaborative demand and supply plans and information between the company and its suppliers. It is agile to meet the responsiveness required by the company's Supply Chain Roadmap; agreed rules manage changes to plans.

c. E-Procurement

E-procurement implementation considers current and planned e-technology developments internally and with suppliers. This understanding is integrated into the company's Information Technology Roadmap.

d. Supply Chain Optimization

Joint programs with key suppliers are in place to remove failure and optimize the Supply Chain. The Velocity Ratio is recognized as a key driver for waste elimination and process acceleration.

e. Environmental Impact

Programs are in place to improve sustainability targets over the product life cycle, including disposal and recycling of material.

f. Resource Allocation

Where joint improvement programs with suppliers require resources, the company has budgeted to make the internal resources available.

g. Skills and Aptitudes of People

The skills, aptitudes, and experience of all people involved are considered when determining their allocation for External Sourcing actions with different supplier categories.

14. Suppliers are fully integrated into the company's Product Management process.

a. Approved Sourcing List

An approved sourcing list exists for priority commodity groups. It has been agreed by Product Management and External Sourcing and is reviewed at appropriate intervals. The process is linked to Material Requirements Planning (MRP) to ensure the use of approved suppliers only.

b. External Sourcing and Product Management Interface

The multi-functional Product Management Team defines the point at which External Sourcing becomes involved.

c. External Sourcing and Supplier Involvement in Ideas and Technology

External Sourcing and supplier involvement may be at the concept design stage for ideation and the adoption of new technology.

d. Supplier Product Development Role

In some circumstances, the supplier may take a full partnership role, with responsibility for developing and supplying technology, products, and services.

BEHAVIORS AND COMPETENCIES

15. **Expressed behaviors define the company, interactions, and responses. The Business Values drives behaviors. There is a clear statement of the ethical standards set between the company and the supplier.**

a. Supplier Review Process

These ethical standards are included as part of the regular supplier review process and are provided to new suppliers.

b. Suppliers' Internal Processes and Cultures

The ways in which the suppliers communicate with and develop their own employees are reviewed and considered in the sourcing decision.

c. Safety, Health, and Environment

The company makes clear to the suppliers its expectation that appropriate and effective safety, health, and environmental standards are in place at the suppliers.

d. Supplier Behavioral Expectations

The behavioral standards expected of suppliers are clear, and processes are in place to ensure that the Values and Guiding Principles of the suppliers are consistent with the company's.

16. **Behavioral characteristics required of those who interface with external suppliers are defined and monitored.**

a. Consistent Behaviors

Supplier Management Leadership may be different among commodity groups but the standards of ethics and behaviors are consistent.

b. Situational Leadership

Leadership is the predominant style; however, Situational Leadership is used as required.

   c. <u>Rewards and Recognition</u>

     Individuals and teams are recognized for their contributions, and team success has become the focus.

   b. <u>Decisiveness</u>

     In the face of uncertainty, decision making is accelerated because of clear lines of authority.

17. Competencies are unique skills, talents, and proficiencies to ensure individual, team, and organizational success.

   a. <u>Leadership</u>

     This is the ability to develop sourcing strategies that provide future advantage, with appropriate sensitivity to emerging social, environmental, and regulatory landscapes.

   b. <u>Execution</u>

     This is functional expertise in supplier selection and sourcing and the negotiation/collaboration competencies during contract development.

   c. <u>Retained Business Expertise</u>

     For outsourced or third-party supply chains, sufficient expertise and resources are retained in-house to effectively maintain oversight and contract management of these goods and services.

PERFORMANCE MEASUREMENT

18. A balanced hierarchy of measures exists to manage and improve External Sourcing processes and supplier performance. All measures have ownership and accountability and are integrated as part of a company suite to drive business improvement.

   a. <u>Balanced Set</u>

     A balanced set of measures supports an optimized sourcing outcome. Collaboration with supplier partners drives understanding that the overall Supply Chain delivery performance is the product of the performance of each step.

   b. <u>Supplier Service Performance</u>

     Supplier performance is measured with both internal and external improvement actions that are agreed. It is recognized that this is typically delivery related for inventory items and customer or plan related for services.

c. Improvement Measures

   The suite of improvement measures, including aspects such as quality performance, documentation accuracy, velocity, safety stock levels, order quantities, lead times, service levels, customer satisfaction, and delivery frequency, is defined, measured, and communicated internally and externally.

d. Quality Assurance

   Quality Assurance standards, goals, and objectives are jointly agreed and documented between the company and its suppliers. The methods of product quality verification, whether on-site or by certification, are defined and agreed.

e. Technical Support Capability

   The supplier's capability in terms of technical support to product and service development or improvement is considered and measured, as appropriate to the commodity group.

19. **Process measures have been defined. These monitor performances that enable the Supply Chain. The specifics of these key performance indicators vary based on business strategy and collaborative agreements.**

a. Supplier Fulfillment Perfect

   Completeness of individual supplier delivery events typically covering quantity, quality, timeliness, and for service items subjective/qualitative behavioral measures are measured and are improving.

b. Supplier Performance to Plan

   Overall performance during an agreed time frame, including response time to change management, is measured and improving. Any gaps in performance relative to established targets are subject to corrective action, and improvement plans are monitored.

c. Supplier Lead Time

   Replenishment time from demand signal to availability is decreasing.

d. Supplier Lead Times for New Product Introduction

   Time to introduce new products or services from gate release to availability is measured and improving.

e. Velocity

   The added-value time as a ratio of total elapsed time for externally sourced supply is measured and is improving in accordance with strategy.

f. Procurement Operations Key Measures

   Procurement performance measures, such as requisitions converted to orders (floor-to-floor time), receipt of goods to payment of invoices within terms, and requisitions fulfilled without manual intervention, are measured relative to established targets and subjected to Continuous Improvement.

20. **Business performance measures for External Sourcing are defined and supported by business-specific measures aligned to the strategy. The standard for each is specified to enable Class A performance and Continuous Improvement.**

   a. Total Cost of Ownership Trend

      The Total Cost of Ownership is being driven down.

   b. Purchased Inventory

      Purchased inventory, including consignment stock, is measured by supplier and is aligned with strategic objectives.

   c. Cost of External Sourcing Operations

      Cost of operations as a percentage of total company fixed and marginal labor costs is measured and reducing.

   d. Effectiveness of External Sourcing Operations

      Total Cost of Ownership or cost of operations of External Sourcing is measured and reducing.

   e. Business Compliance

      Goods and services bought through compliant acquisition channels expressed as a percentage of value and percentage of transactions are monitored relative to established targets. Gaps to targets are subject to corrective action and are regularly reviewed.

OLIVER WIGHT BIOGRAPHY

Oliver Wight was a pioneer in planning processes. Ollie recognized the problems faced by companies and had a clear understanding of their needs. He was always looking to the future and finding ways to improve things.

Oliver Wight had two great gifts. He could take complicated subjects, unravel them, and make them simple.

More important, he had a sensitivity to people that broke down barriers. He had innovative ideas and could communicate them in a way that gained acceptance, commitment, and enthusiasm.

Somehow, in the early years of the computer revolution, the role of people was misplaced. Ollie  made it his personal mission to put people back where they belong and to give them the understanding they need to use their new tools. Among his many enduring tenets is, "Computers are not the key to success, people are." This remains a core philosophy of The Oliver Wight Companies.

Oliver Wight used his gifts to build an enduring legacy in business processes. Nearly every company using planning processes and Ollie's philosophies, passed on through teaching, writing, and consulting, experienced significant increases in productivity, inventory turnover, customer service, and growth.

His emphasis on the people side of business solutions earned him a reputation as a leading thinker in business education.

Ollie once said, quite modestly, "I've left some footprints." Those who have chosen to follow them are better off both personally and professionally.

Oliver Wight was 53 years old when he passed away in 1983.